Silent Music

SILENT MUSIC

The Life, Work, and Thought
of St. John of the Cross

R. A. Herrera

WILLIAM B. EERDMANS PUBLISHING COMPANY
GRAND RAPIDS, MICHIGAN / CAMBRIDGE, U.K.

© 2004 Wm. B. Eerdmans Publishing Co.

Wm. B. Eerdmans Publishing Co.
255 Jefferson Ave. S.E., Grand Rapids, Michigan 49503 /
P.O. Box 163, Cambridge CB3 9PU U.K.

Printed in the United States of America

08 07 06 05 04   7 6 5 4 3 2 1

Library of Congress Cataloging-in-Publication Data

Herrera, Robert A.
Silent music: the life, work, and thought of St. John of the Cross / R. A. Herrera.
p.   cm.
Includes bibliographical references and index.
ISBN 0-8028-2495-1 (alk. paper)
1. John of the Cross, Saint, 1542-1591.   I. Title.
BX4700.J7H398   2004
271′.7302 — dc22
[B]

2003064342

www.eerdmans.com

To the memory of
Fray Hilario del Niño Jesús, OCD,
and Fray Otilio Rodriguez, OCD,
who introduced me to St. John of the Cross's
work, spirit, and manner of life

Contents

Acknowledgments

I wish to express my appreciation to those whose kindness and expertise contributed to the completion of this work: Ed Garea, who made valuable suggestions; my wife Deborah and her able staff at the Seton Hall University Law Library; Andrew Hoogheem, Eerdmans' editor, who labored to turn the original dross into gossamer.

Mysticism

I

Mysticism is a protean term used to signify a variety of disparate phenomena from the sublime to the trivial, from the effusions of the God-intoxicated saint to the babblings of the hallucinogen-intoxicated addict. It runs the gamut from St. Teresa's mansions of the soul to Timothy Leary's neural cocoon. Discrimination is required to distinguish between the genuine and the spurious article.

Mystical states and their counterfeits have been produced in a multiplicity of ways: prayer, meditation, speculation, logic, numbers, letters, music, bodily postures, drugs, breathing techniques. Perhaps because of this very breadth, 'mysticism' has been used as a term of reproach for opinions considered vague, vast, eccentric, or bizarre; without basis in either fact or reason. William James, in his *Varieties of Religious Experience*,[1] catalogues a veritable menagerie of mystical and mystical-like phenomena. As he maintained that the unconscious — in his vocabulary the 'transmarginal' — provides the 'door' to the mysti-

---

1. William James, *Varieties of Religious Experience* (New York: Modern Library, 1922), 370-71.

cal, it follows that mysticism is closely allied to psychopathology, a truth that has been accepted by the most acute of spiritual guides.

It cannot be denied that the psychotic hallucinations of Freud's patient Schreber[2] and the outlandish accounts of some mystics have a family resemblance. Lord Russell, with his usual malice, quipped: "From a scientific point of view, we can make no distinction between a man who eats little and sees heaven and a man who drinks much and sees snakes."[3] This is both an acerbic and a humorous indictment of mysticism, and a clue to the inability of a certain cast of mind to deal with the phenomenon. It insists on documentation and research, a justification which mysticism cannot provide as this would imprison it within the natural order. One cannot compare secular apples and celestial oranges.

Although mysticism is a puzzle it should be kept in mind that its often exotic language and the bizarre phenomena associated with it hinge on a single point: If God exists — and the consensus of the Mystics of the Book (that is, the followers of Judaism, Christianity, Islam) believe that He does — then God is the ultimate goal of human life. Moreover, He is a goal which humankind cannot attain by its efforts alone. Divine aid is necessary. The conviction that the beatific vision is grounded on God, the *lumen gloriae* of the theologians, delivered Christianity from becoming no more than another priggish intellectual sect or esoteric mystery religion.

It has been said that the mystic exemplifies Divine generosity in a unique manner. The reception of God's grace, often in an experiential mode, allows the mystic to see more clearly, to expand the boundaries of reality. In "A Crazy Tale," a delightful piece written by G. K. Chesterton, the protagonist states:[4]

---

2. Schreber was convinced that he was dead, decomposing, but yet in direct communication with God (among other absurdities). Sigmund Freud, *The Complete Works of Sigmund Freud*, ed. James Strachey (London: The Hogarth Press, 1971), 20:3-84.

3. Bertrand Russell, *Religion and Science* (London: Routledge, 1935), 188.

4. G. K. Chesterton, *Daylight and Nightmare. Uncollected Stories and Fables*, selected by Marie Smith (New York: Dodd, Mead & Co., 1986), 21.

I am the first that ever saw the world. Prophets and Sages there have been out of whose great hearts came schools and churches. But I am the first who ever saw a dandelion as it is.

Once the distance that separates him from the mystic is admitted, and the playful tone dismissed, this presents a fair analogy if not a real approximation to the experience of the mystic. Several Church Fathers taught that the world of things which assault our senses are only the degenerate forms of that beautiful and luminous original creation which was muddied by the Fall. It can be said that the mystic claims to be able to penetrate the carapace of the external world, view the beauty within, and ascend to its source, the "all-beautiful One" of St. Augustine.[5] That the mystic is directed towards this vision is often lost in the horrifying penances and bizarre exotica that glut their accounts.

2

The first glimmerings of mysticism can be found in primitive societies. Perhaps it was incubated by a chilling awareness of the fragile human condition, perhaps prodded by nostalgia for wholeness, the aspiration of repairing the chasm between earth and the lost paradise. Mircea Eliade indicates that the rites and techniques practiced to repair this break comprise what more highly developed religions consider to be mysticism.[6] These rites and techniques endeavor to erase the boundaries of space and time, to bridge the chasm separating earth and paradise.

Closer at hand are the Greek mysteries such as the Eleusinian, the Orphic and the Dionysian. They featured rites that were kept secret except to the initiates, who were trained to receive the revelation under the guidance of a hierophant. What might be called Greek "mysticism" consisted in the search for a more direct, a more intimate contact with

5. *Sermon on John* 10.13.

6. Mircea Eliade, *Myths, Dreams and Realities* (New York: Harper, 1960), 43ff.; *Images and Symbols* (New York: Sheed & Ward, 1961), 54.

3

the gods. As Aristotle indicated, the initiates did not endeavor to acquire knowledge but to experience emotions and attain a certain state of mind.[7] The Dionysian rites featured the intoxication of *ekstasis,* literally a "stepping out," appropriate to the god of 'mania' or divine madness invoked by Hesiod and Pindar as "the cause of happiness." This introduced an experience foreign to that of the official cult.

The majestic figures of the Old Testament such as Moses, Isaiah, and Elijah were incorporated into the bloodstream of Christianity as the New Israel, testifying to truly unique encounters with God: the ascent to YHWH on the summit of Sinai; the prophet overcome by the bitterness of his own nothingness; the theophany of a gentle breeze. All were considered by early Christians to be types or prefigurations of their faith's mysticism. Indeed, the Hebrew Bible was a source of inspiration for all three Religions of the Book.

3

The view articulated by Harnack that "mysticism is always the same . . . there are no national or confessional distinctions,"[8] is erroneous, though at one time it was widely held, perhaps the product of exacerbated romanticism, or of a desire to put all the religious eccentrics into one category, into a single asylum. A glimpse at Judaism, Christianity, and Islam indicates that they embraced often similar, but often wildly different, types of spirituality. The divergences between Abraham Abulafia, Meister Eckhart, and Ibn 'Arabi are many and deep. And this is only a random sampling. It could be expanded into a veritable catalogue of ships.

Perhaps the most important similarity between the religions, aside from superficial parallels (as, for example, Christian monasticism, the loosely knit Islamic communities, and the master-student relation

---

7. Jean-Pierre Vernant, "Greek Religion," in *Religions of Antiquity,* ed. Robert M. Seltzer (New York: Macmillan, 1989), 182-83.

8. Adolph von Harnack, *History of Dogma* (New York: Dover, 1961), 7:97.

in Judaism exemplified by the Hasidic Rebbe) is their grounding on canonical texts. Aside from the Hebrew Bible these differ widely. Christian mysticism looks to the Gospels and to the Epistles, Judaism to a number of texts headed by the Zohar, and Islam to a spiritual reading of the Qur'an.

The adepts of Kabbalah believed that it presented the authentic tradition of Judaism. The Zohar came to be considered a sacred text third only to the Hebrew Bible and the Talmud, at one time surpassing even the latter in authority. The Zohar is not a single unified work but a great literary anthology attributed to Rabbi Simeon ben Yohai though probably the work of Rabbi Moses de León.[9] It reached the height of its influence in seventeenth-century Safed, the Kabbalah elaborated by Rabbi Isaac Luria and his circle. The Latin translation by Knorr von Rosenroth, *Kabbalah desnudata* (1677), exercised some influence on Christian circles, including the great Leibniz.

In Islam mysticism had its source in Muhammad himself, who, in spite of his strong condemnation of Christian monasticism, endorsed, possibly due to the example of the Hanifs, such practices as prayer, vigils, and fasting. Sufism took up Qur'anic terms such as *dhika* (praise of God) and *tawakkul* (trust in God) and developed them, possibly influenced by Christianity, in a spiritual — even a mystical — direction. The female ascetic, Rabi'a of Basra, elaborated a theory of mystical love and Abu Yazid of Bistami developed the doctrine of *fana* (annihilation) some two centuries or so after the death of the Prophet. Sufi spirituality gave birth to rules of discipline and devotional manuals of theory and practice. When Al-Ghazali (1058-1111) provided Sufism with a philosophical justification, mystical revelation took its place together with tradition and reason as a fundamental principle of Islamic faith.

The center of Christian spirituality is provided by the canonical accounts of the life of Jesus and by the Pauline Epistles. While the Synoptic Gospels emphasize the proclamation of the Kingdom, the Gospel

---

9. An excellent presentation to the Zohar and a discussion as to authorship are found in *The Wisdom of the Zohar: An Anthology of Text*, arr. F. Lachover and I. Tishby, trans. David Goldstein (London: Littman Library / Oxford U. Press, 1991) I:13-25.

of John stresses such categories as life, light, love, and spirit, which seems to justify its reputation as the "charter" of Christian mysticism. And this in spite of its decided intellectualistic, abstractive tilt noted by von Hugel[10] — despite which, the mystical theme found in the prologue links up with the final words of the third chapter of II Corinthians:[11]

> we all reflect as in a mirror the splendor of the Lord; thus we are transfigured into his likeness, from splendor to splendor; such is the influence of the Lord who is Spirit.

Christian mystical theology, not as yet distinguished from the ascetic, seems to have had its origin with the Alexandrians Clement and Origen, continuing with Evagrius Ponticus and Gregory of Nyssa, over a period that spans about two hundred years. It was Athanasius' *Life of Antony* which, according to Gregory Nazianzen, provided the "pattern" of what a monk ought to be. Moreover, it was Gregory who, in his *Homilies on the Canticle* uses for the first time "mystical contemplation" in the sense of spiritual experience.[12] Plotinus had previously spoken of "ecstasy" as losing oneself in the One.[13]

It was approximately during the fourth century, as Dom Leclercq has indicated, that the Greek word *monachos* gave birth to the Latin *monachus*. The 'monos' is a Christian who is, at least to some extent, a solitary.[14] It was out of this background that mysticism reached a watershed in the elusive person of the Pseudo-Denis whose reputation was authenticated by St. Maximus. He was influenced by Neoplato-

---

10. C. P. M. Jones, "The New Testament," in *The Study of Spirituality,* ed. C. Jones, G. Wainwright, and E. Yarnold, SJ (New York: Oxford U. Press, 1986), 84.

11. II Corinthians 3:18f. (NET).

12. Louis Bouyer, *The Christian Mystery,* trans. Illtyd Trethowan (Edinburgh: T&T Clark, 1990), 173, 177.

13. Plotinus *Enneads* VI.9.11. Refer to the MacKenna translation (London: Faber & Faber, 1956).

14. Dom Jean Leclercq, OSB, *Aux Sources de la Spiritualité Occidentale* (Paris: Editions du Cerf, 1964), 16.

nism and was accorded subapostolic authority as he was mistakenly identified as Denis the Areopagite, the convert of St. Paul. Possibly a Syrian monk of the fifth century or so, the three treatises and ten letters attributed to him became the shaky scaffolding on with much of future mystical theory would rest.

This kaleidoscopic tradition was introduced into the West by Cassian (+435), who regarded contemplation as arising from meditation on the Scriptures. It melded with the Augustinian tradition and reached Pope St. Gregory (+604) in an attenuated form that filtered down to the Victorines and St. Bernard, among many others. With Meister Eckhart (+1327), the Dionysian inspiration peaked in intensity only to lose impetus and be found in more domesticated forms in the Rhineland mystics. This passes on to Spain and ultimately to St. John of the Cross.

4

The mystic has been portrayed as a person who has fallen in love with God, as a psychotic, an Epicurean, a romantic, a voluptuary, a psychologist, a nihilist, and more. All this in spite of his oddities, the aura of otherworldliness that surrounds him, and his ramblings along little-used paths. But the mystic is not a dreamer or a self-inflated psychopath. His point of departure is a hard-nosed appraisal of the human condition; his method some type of moral or spiritual purification to rectify its failings. His goal: proximity to or union with, the highest reality. The heterodox mystic may believe that he — his inner self — is divine; the orthodox would not labor under such a dangerous illusion. The mystic's quest has been compared to a path to be traversed, a bridge to be crossed, a ladder to be mounted, a height to be scaled, a cloud to be entered.

Regarding the Christian mystic — this being the subject of the present work — divine grace must be mentioned. It is the principle of Christian life. Grace usually dwells silently in the human soul and is nurtured by an ascetic life of prayer and self-discipline. It allows the soul to participate in the Divine Life and leads it to the vision of God. Following this path the soul can reach the very highest levels of sanctity.

The mystical life is different. In the mystical life grace develops in a mode that surpasses the natural order and, to some extent at least, is experiential. It elevates the soul to a degree of infused knowledge and love, which at its apex is identified as mystical contemplation. The weird and odd, the gamut of isolated phenomena in which spiritual accounts abound, no matter how elevated, do not make a mystical life. These phenomena must be integrated, must respond to a principle of organization, must form a structure, an organism, to be so identified.

Everyday life is the necessary point of departure for the mystical, which claims, unlike everyday life, to transcend space, time, and conceptual thought. It aspires to bring about an enlargement of the soul, attain a higher level of consciousness. Everyday life, structured by the ascetic, becomes open to the mystical. Asceticism found its Christian institutional expression in monasticism, which was initiated in quasi-organized form, with the communities founded by Pachomius, near Dendera, during the reign of Constantine.

The Desert Fathers had no program, no timetable. Their lives were grounded on the master-disciple relationship and, more importantly, on the monastic cell, considered to be the supreme teacher. In silence and solitude the struggle against Satan, whose presence was considered to be especially strong in the desert, and against the self, was waged. There were, however, different paths to arrive at the fear of God and purity of heart. While Antony preached complete withdrawal from the world, Pachomius tilted towards community and organization.

Clement of Alexandria moved further along the path to a more elevated spirituality when he appropriated the Stoic discipline of *apatheia* (indifference) as a means to augment the soul's capacity for *agape* (Christian love). His pupil, Origen, taught that asceticism dealt with restoring the divine image in humankind, that it was an aspect of the universal *apokatastasis* (recapitulation) that restores the divine image to creation. Augustine, about a century later, inaugurates a new approach in Christian spirituality by melding asceticism with the noetic flights and experiences of the Neoplatonists. Christians with intellectual baggage may ascend to God by means of Christ and still enjoy the experiences of the Neoplatonists.[15]

The desert did not disappear, but with the passing years it was transferred to the human soul. Augustine, writing to Nebridius, urges withdrawal from the world. Seek refuge in the privacy of the soul. In a sermon, he advises:[16]

> Enter into yourself, and leave behind all the noise and confusion . . . some delightful hidden place in your consciousness where you can be free of noise and argument. . . . Hear the word in quietness, that you may understand it.

Centuries later, within the monasteries, a similar transposition will take place, from the physical pilgrimage to the interior pilgrimage, the *peregrinatio in stabilitate*.

Monasticism in the West was dominated by St. Benedict of Nursia (+547) and the Rule attributed to him. This attempt to "establish a school for the service of the Lord" had lasting repercussions. Southern indicates that "the Benedictine Rule had a monopoly in Western Europe from the early eighth century to the middle of the eleventh when its hold on the mind and affections of the whole population seemed to be complete."[17] The Rule endeavored to establish barriers against all deviations. It stigmatized the rootless, wandering monk as a 'gyrovague' — following in the wake of Augustine, who himself castigated the long-haired eccentrics that hawked spurious relics.[18] Monasticism, as with any other institution, had its periods of relaxation and those of reformation. Responding to the criticisms of Peter Damien in the eleventh century, the Camaldoli foun-

15. My "Augustine: A Spiritual Centaur?" in *Augustine: Mystic and Mystagogue,* ed. Frederick Van Fleteren, Joseph C. Schnaubelt, OSA, and Joseph Reino (New York: Peter Lang, 1994), 159-76.

16. *Sermo* 52.22.

17. J. A. McGuckin, "Christian Asceticism and the Early School of Alexandria," in *Monks, Hermits and the Monastic Tradition,* ed. W. J. Sheils (London: Blackwell, 1985), 25.

18. *St. Benedict's Rule for Monsteries,* trans. L. J. Doyle (Collegeville, Minn.: The Liturgical Press, 1948), ch. 1.

dation was developed on the pattern of the ancient *laura*. Returning to the ideal of the eremitic life the monks, in isolation from the world and in silence, endeavored to forge an intense spiritual life.

The ascetic life was often pushed to an extreme. The border between rugged spirituality and psychopathology often became blurred. This might have been the case with La Trappe under de Rance (+1700). Far worse, the growth of a malevolent double within Christian spirituality, perhaps initiated with Elymas, the sorcerer struck blind by St. Paul (Acts 13:4-12), continued to fester in heretical sects of all persuasions, especially those of antinomian hue. These two faces of spirituality were reflected in Gorres's *Mystik*, a nineteenth-century product in which two volumes of divine mysticism are followed by two volumes of diabolical mysticism.[19]

5

Mystical contemplation is a hybrid term evidencing a marriage of East and West. Mysticism is derived from Eastern Christianity, contemplation from Western Christianity. When juxtaposed, each points to a complementary aspect of a single reality: mysticism to its intellectual and contemplation to its practical and voluntaristic. While Gregory of Nyssa speaks of penetrating the invisible and incomprehensible, Pope Gregory I speaks of the tasting of unencompassed truth.[20] The terms became almost convertible. With the advantage of chronological priority, mysticism passes into the West through Scotus Eriugena's translations of Pseudo-Denis's works.

The Pseudo-Denis provided mysticism with an idiom, an ideology, and a framework. It reached Augustine through the *Libri platonici* and the translations of Marius Victorinus. The influence of the *Corpus Areopagiticum* was immense, slowly working its way into the secular

19. Dom Cuthbert Butler, OSB, *Western Mysticism* (London: Arrow, 1960), 186.

20. *From Glory to Glory: Texts from Gregory of Nyssa's Mystical Writings*, ed. Jean Daniélou and Herbert Musurillo (New York: Scribners, 1961), 21. Pope Gregory I, *Moralia* V.66.

realm more than a millennium later through the philosophies of German Idealism. Following Augustine was Pope Gregory I, who advised that "stillness" was the royal road to contemplation, indicating that prior to vision there is a *"visio per appetitum."*[21] However, he veered away from the Dionysian apophatic theology of darkness, cloud, and ray of darkness to a theology of boundless light.

Mysticism distinguished itself from religion proper by claiming to teach a deeper mystery, to unveil a hidden meaning. It held out the promise of experiencing, "tasting," the hidden truth, of attaining knowledge surpassing intellectual cognition, of enjoying a foretaste of the beatific vision. Plato, in the *Republic* and the *Symposium*,[22] provides accounts of the ascent of the soul to reality. The first ascent is intellectual and arrives at *noesis* (insight). There the soul comes into contact with the World of Ideas, rising to the highest reality, the Idea of the Good. The ascent described in the *Symposium* is erotic, reaching the Idea of the Beautiful. The influence of these elevations upon Christian theology was substantial, in spite of their frank opposition to Christian spirituality which, insisting on Divine initiative and concurrence, disallows all types of self-propelled ascents to the highest reality.

Spirituality is both individual (private prayer) and corporate (liturgy). However, the mystical charism (exceptional events such as Pentecost to one side) seems to be the privilege of individuals. The Old Testament is dominated by the collective, the corporate. Even the psalms, which are ostensibly individual, are personifications of the community. This corporate tilt passes from the Old to the New Testament, from the Old to the New Israel, together with the majestic themes of the awesome character, the hiddenness, and the presence of God.

In medieval monasticism the divine office, the *opus dei,* was the center of community life, yet Benedict allowed a place to private prayer, even within the office itself. Prayer should be brief, he taught,

---

21. Dom Jean Leclercq, OSB, "From St. Gregory to St. Bernard," in *The Spirituality of the Middle Ages,* ed. F. Bouyer, J. Leclercq, and F. Vandenbroucke (London: Burns and Oates, 1968), 10-13. Bouyer, *op. cit.,* 225.

22. *Republic* 588b-621d, *Symposium* 209e-212c.

unless it happens to be prolonged by "an inspiration of divine grace."[23] It is this "inspiration" that provides a point of departure for contemplative prayer, for mystical contemplation. It should be noted that, as Dom Leclercq indicates, the problem concerning the liturgical cult and intimate (private) prayer did not exist in medieval monasticism. It arises later in modernity with the evolution of the cult of intimate prayer.[24] As no hard line existed between vocal, mental and liturgical prayer each passing instant provided an opportunity for the operations of grace.

In the liturgy the worshipper confesses to God both as an individual and as the representative of the entire creation. In private prayer the worshipper occupies, as an image of the Image, a place in which, to borrow from Newman, *"cor ad cor loquitur."* Exacerbations of both can and have led to upsets: the private to the apotheosis of the individual, the common to the annihilation of the individual. A sane spirituality attempts to steer between the imperial ego and the anthill.

6

The Renaissance put an end to the medieval worldview and furthered the mystagogic to the detriment of the mystical. Campanella and Bruno, more *magi* than philosophers or theologians, were representative. Obsession with Hermes Trismegistus, and the *prisca theologica* even burgeoned in the greatest thinker of the dawning age. Nicholas of Cusa (+1464) wrote a popular version of his great work *De Docta Ignorantia* called *De visione dei,* which sets forth "an easy path" to mystical contemplation.[25] Although this work could be considered to be the equivalent of contemporary devotional manuals, its substance and depth show that it decidedly is not. It also shows that even in a period in which the lure of Paganism was at its strongest and most irresistible, Christian mysticism was still able to show some signs of life.

23. *Rule,* ch. 73.
24. Leclercq, *Spirituality,* 285.
25. Edward Yarnold, "Nicholas of Cusa," in *The Study of Spirituality,* 327.

The mystics of Germany and Holland have been represented as precursors of the Protestant Reformation. This is certainly true in part. But Protestantism did not treat its precursors kindly, causing a break if not a scuttling of the mystical tradition. The tremendous personality of Martin Luther (+1546) recapitulated the voices that, throughout centuries, had been raised against the perceived corruptions and injustices of Rome. As Harnack stated, "Luther attacked the whole Catholic (not only the medieval) ideal of Christian perfection."[26] The ancient piety fell victim to the juggernaut of *sola fide*.

Luther assailed asceticism in *Judgment on Monastic Vows* and mysticism in the person of the Pseudo-Denis in *The Pagan Servitude of the Church.* The Christian, he counsels, should not give the least weight to these books: "So far from learning about Christ you will be led to lose what you know."[27] This marked a change in attitude from his youth when he meditated on the Song of Songs and believed himself to have received an experience of a mystical nature. This early inclination was muted by the 'totally unmystical' conviction that trust in God *propter Christum* was the authentic content of religion.[28]

Gibbon, in his magisterial *Decline and Fall of the Roman Empire* (1776-1788) reflects the hardening of these views within Protestantism. Twenty pages of the thirty-seventh chapter dedicated to the monks explodes with vitriol. Monasticism is identified with superstition, fanaticism, and degeneracy. In Chadwick's words it is "one of the most strident specimens of sustained invective and cold hatred to be found in English prose."[29] (Perhaps the warmed-over resentment bred by Gibbon's youthful conversion to Catholicism?) It may be countered that the exacerbations of the Counter-Reformation proved that the bitter fruits of *odium theologicum* were found on both sides of the struggle.

What had occurred? The Protestant present had been separated

26. Harnack, *op. cit.*, 7:215.

27. "The Pagan Servitude of the Church," in *Martin Luther: Selections from His Writings*, ed. John Dillenberger (New York: Doubleday Anchor, 1951), 342-43.

28. Harnack, *op. cit.*, 7:183.

29. Henry Chadwick, "The Ascetic Ideal in the History of the Church," in *Monks, Hermits and the Ascetic Tradition,* ed. W. J. Sheils (Oxford: Blackwell, 1986), 6.

from the Catholic past. The mass, the saints, monasticism were abolished; the theology of the exception and mysticism were replaced by corporate religion and pietism. Mysticism was obliged to retreat to the hinterlands and take strange and grotesque shapes even when found in the groves of Academe. Henry More (+1687) was much influenced by Kabbalah. Jakob Boehme (+1624) was more of a theosophist than a mystic, elaborating the notion of a divine world-creating contraction, a theory which greatly resembled the Kabbalistic *zimzum* and maintained that evil is rooted in an aspect of the Divine Nature.[30] The fascinating genius of William Blake (+1827) tilted in a similar direction. His version of God as "Nobodaddy" has deep roots in Gnosticism and his unfinished poem, *The Everlasting Gospel* shows the influence of Gnostic as well as Joachite sources.[31]

After the shattering of Christendom and the luxuriant spiritual autumn of the Counter-Reformation Roman Catholics became less inclined or less capable of scaling the highest peaks of spirituality and slumped into the professorial, the parochial, and the fantastic. Modernity, characterized by chatter, clutter, and control, set up a barrier to authentic spirituality that has been very difficult to overcome. The muse was closeted within the privacy of the contemplative cells and the secret chambers of privileged souls. Nevertheless, there have been striking examples of the mystical charism in souls such as Elizabeth de la Trinité, Thérèse of Lisieux, Edith Stein, and others.

Orthodox mysticism is multicolored. Because of its long tradition and the romantic aura it has acquired over the centuries, the medieval variety has been popular with both literary persons and scholars. However, misconceptions have been rife. T. S. Eliot, for example, favored the twelfth-century mysticism of Richard of St. Victor (+1176) which he identifies (in my opinion erroneously) with the mysticism of Dante, which he believed originated in Aristotle's *Metaphysics*.[32] He discerns

---

30. Andrew Weeks, *Boehme* (Albany: State University of New York Press, 1995), 1-12; 232, n. 23.

31. G. L. Keyes, "William Blake," in *Encyclopaedia Britannica*, 14th ed. (1929), III:695a-696b.

32. T. S. Eliot, *The Varieties of Mystical Poetry* (New York: Harcourt, Brace, 1994), 99. The reference is to *Metaphysics* 1072b.

two great divisions among the mystics: the Aristotelian-Victorine-Dantesque, which is classical and ontological, and the Spanish, which is romantic and psychological.[33] Although the twelfth century is a good point of departure as it represents a transition from the outer to the inner pilgrimage, Eliot's observations should be accepted with care. It should be noted that these "mystics" represent only a minor fragment of a vast tapestry.

Though he himself was scarcely a mystic, it has been suggested that in an age of burgeoning secularism, Cervantes' *Don Quixote* can be said to exemplify the mystic spirit. Like the mystic he strives to vanquish, even to destroy, that which fallen nature considers being most valuable, even life itself, to attain a life that is more real, intense and lasting.[34] This entails, at least in spirit, regression to the Gothic, the medieval, and has been emulated by moderns and contemporaries, notably (but not solely) by the followers of St. Ignatius Loyola and St. Teresa of Ávila. But even these have suffered greatly from the slough of despond that followed the Second Vatican Council.

7

In Protestantism the barrier to mystical theology was far more difficult to overcome. The worshipper appeared to be hermetically sealed within the religious community, itself usually an appendage of the State. Voices such as Søren Kierkegaard (+1855) were heard within the deadening correctness. This hypersensitive aesthete came to the conclusion that Denmark's State-sponsored orthodoxy was merely cordial drivel served up sweet.[35] The corporate, he feared, was suffocating the individual. This was a real tragedy as the cause of Christ stands or falls

33. *Ibid.*, 104.

34. David Rubio, OSA, *La Filosofía del Quijote* (Buenos Aires: Editorial Losada, 1943), 46-47.

35. *Provocations: Spiritual Writings of Kierkegaard*, comp. and ed. Charles E. Moore (Farmington, Penn.: The Plough Pub. Co., 1999), 16-17.

with the individual. The task at hand is to become a unique self, to escape from the herd and its mentality.[36]

Kierkegaard embraces the ascetic by his either/or: either God or nothing! He moves in the direction of the mystical by his advocacy of silence as the essence of inwardness. The imperatives of the monastic cell are reborn: "It is unbelievable what a person of prayer can achieve if he would but close the doors behind him."[37] It is interesting to note that less than two decades or so later the archetypal atheist Nietzsche (+1900) was also engaged in excoriating the masses and their herd mentality.

Both Don Quixote and Kierkegaard, the fictional character and the existent man (who can say which is the more real?) kicked against the goad. They were in frank opposition to that stultifying conformity that all too often passes for religion. Kierkegaard sacrificed his love for Regina; Don Quixote fought giants that to secular eyes were merely windmills. From a psychiatric point of view both were verging on the borderline or had passed the border into psychosis. Kierkegaard made the sacrifice necessary to make his vocation possible. Don Quixote fought against the windmills of Criptana, as he knew through the eyes of faith that they were, are, and for all eternity will be, giants. In their realization that the demands and lures of the world must be subordinated to a higher calling they were well on their way to an elevated spirituality.

8

St. John of the Cross (+1591) was a mystic who professed orthodoxy and received the highest honors from the Catholic Church as saint and Doctor. Though he has also been perceived as a nihilist and a Buddhist, it would be more to the point to simply say he was an anti-Prometheus in a Promethean Age, born in an epoch characterized by the affirma-

36. *Ibid.*, 21-24.
37. *Ibid.*, 18, 348, 374.

tion of the world and nature, by the expression of secular joy.[38] This was the age of Justus Lipsius, Giordano Bruno, Galileo, Campanella, and Francis Bacon; a world that found its highest expression in the gospel of infinite nature. In the presence of this triumphant secularism, John of the Cross appeared to deprecate both humanity and nature as cumbersome baggage in his pursuit of a distant and unfamiliar God. He was not a philosopher or a theologian in a professional sense, but a man inebriated with God to whom everything else was of little or no importance.

Austin Farrer suggested that no person knows what to do with the divine when it falls into their hands;[39] this is certainly true of St. John, whose life was a heroic attempt to assimilate and to be assimilated by the Divine. The mystic is the proverbial one-eyed man in the country of the blind. He sees more but in a woefully deficient manner. If Aquinas is correct in affirming that *"omnis intellectus naturaliter desiderat substantiae visionem,"*[40] the mystic is the vicar of humanity in exploring an uncharted territory, one who in this life may enjoy a foretaste of the next. The surreal canvases of El Greco (+1614) have been called the complement to the poems of St. John of the Cross.[41] The rhythmic elongated figures, the twisted limbs, the all-too-brilliant whites and reds that impressed St. Teresa, the supernatural world bursting out of the natural by a weird geometry, correspond to the saint's religious vision. His favorite images: night, flame, darkness, lamps of fire, the cross. A man of poetic genius and psychological insight, his humility and extraordinary patience in suffering were most unusual in an age busy discarding the inner life for that of the secular.

St. John of the Cross has much to teach us, especially as a guide to the alien regions of the spirit. Firmly rooted in the Christian tradition he also forms part of a unique fragment of Spanish history. Both require some elaboration. A study of his life and times may serve as both

38. Refer to Wilhelm Dilthey, *Hombre y Mundo en los Siglos XVI y XVII* (Mexico: Fondo de Cultura Económica, 1947), 438.

39. Austin Farrer, *The Glass of Vision* (Westminster: Dacre Press, 1966), 139.

40. *Summa Contra Gentiles* III.57; cf. III.50.

41. Maurice Barrès, *Greco ou le Secret de Toledo* (Paris: Plon, 1924), 136.

an introduction to the elevated life of the spirit and as an antidote to the depredations of an inglorious era already well on its way to losing both its memory and its God.

CHAPTER ONE

The Setting

No life can be understood in a vacuum. Individuals are known only in relation to their backgrounds. A life must be viewed within a framework that exhibits a multiplicity of factors: the historical, the religious, the sociological. The life of St. John of the Cross presents special difficulties as its backdrop is (to contemporary readers) both captivating and strangely alien. In words that were uttered during the Spanish Civil War, García Morente observed that the Spanish conception of life is grounded on the superiority of the concrete over the abstract, the individual over the species, and the private over the public.[1] This was no less true for the sixteenth century than it is for today.

Spanish mysticism tilts to action rather than speculation, experience rather than abstraction. One recalls Hilaire Belloc's astonishment at hearing the *Salve Regina* sung in a small Spanish village: harsh, full of battle and agony, strikingly different from anything he previously experienced.[2] The same attitude is reflected in Miguel de Unamuno's

1. Manuel García Morente, *Idea de la Hispanidad* (Madrid: Espasa-Calpe, 1961), 91f.

2. "The Relic," in *Hilaire Belloc: Selected Essays*, ed. J. B. Norton (Baltimore: Penguin, 1958), 82-83.

preference for the "Spanish Christ," livid, squalid, bruised, bloody, and ferocious:[3]

> Yes, there is a triumphant, glorious, celestial Christ: the Christ of the transfiguration, the ascension, the Christ who sits at the right hand of the Father . . . this is when we have triumphed. . . . But here . . . in this life which is nothing but a tragic spectacle, here the other Christ, the livid, the bruised, the bloody.

This notion of life as a tragic spectacle, life as the bullring writ large, is etched indelibly on the Spanish psyche. This taste for high drama, exaggeration, extremism in all its forms, is found in a heightened form in the monarchs, warriors, poets, and mystics of Spain's *Edad de Oro* (Golden Age). Its mysticism is ardent and militant, an affirmation of the power of a will that surrenders only to a higher, transcendent will. This irascible Christianity displaced knighthood from the military battlefield to the higher battlefield of the spirit prodded by that *"divina extravagancia"* and *"feliz locura"* which persuaded humankind to forget the world and live completely for God.

This enthusiasm for divine chivalry inspired works such as *La Caballería Celeste* and *La Caballería Cristiana*. Combined with the strong attraction exercised by both the New World and the "Indies of the Spirit," this fervor blunted the impact on Spain of the hermetic aspect of the Renaissance and the Protestant Reformation. The cultural explosion of the Golden Age marched to the beat of a different drummer. Though perhaps rightly accused of being the only region in Europe choosing the past over the present, Spain kept the colorful brilliance of the Catholic festival and did not succumb to the lure either of the classical past or of the cold and denuded churches of the north.

*   *   *

3. Miguel de Unamuno, *Mi religión y otros ensayos* (Madrid: Espasa-Calpe, 1968), 29, 33.

The reign of the Catholic Ferdinand and Isabella provided the spectacular backdrop for the world of St. John of the Cross. This epoch-making reign witnessed the union of Castile and Aragón, the conquest of Granada and Naples, the pacification of Castile, the establishment of the Inquisition, the reform of the clergy, the expulsion of the Jews, and the discovery of the New World. The course of Spanish, European, and world history was greatly affected. In spite of differing views, their reign was neither a paradise subsequently lost nor a season in hell, though it displayed characteristics of both.

The union of Castile and Aragón, marking the birth of modern Spain, was at first more of a personal than a political union. There existed marked divergences that were slow in melding. The two regions were, and to a certain extent still are, dissimilar, even antithetical. While Aragon looked to the Mediterranean, focusing on Italy and France, Castile looked to Portugal, Africa and (after 1492) the New World. Aragon was oriented towards city life, placing great importance on civic virtue, civic rights, and trade. Castilians had a notoriously low opinion of cities, and of trade and all its accessories. The Castilian maxim "Laws obey Kings" was countered by the *Fueros de Aragon,* which declared that "Kings obey Laws."[4] These regional differences were reflected in the characters of Ferdinand and Isabella, who were able to subordinate their differences to form an effective unity.

Ferdinand, at the age of twelve, received his baptism of fire at Calaf with an impressive victory. Under the tutelage of his redoubtable parents he easily scaled the heights of prominence. Isabella, conversely, was pursued by ill fortune. Her mother lapsed into insanity. Her half-brother, Henry IV of Castile, was weak, ineffective, and depraved.[5] She was obliged to painfully wend her way through a maze of plots and counterplots, dealing with courtiers, warriors, prelates, perverts, toadies, and schemers of all varieties. Over the years she found herself be-

4. J. N. Hillgarth, *The Spanish Kingdoms 1250-1517* (Oxford: Clarendon Press, 1978), 2:626.

5. *Historia de España,* ed. Ramón Menéndez Pidal (Madrid: Espasa-Calpe, 1969), 17.I.x, xxvi.

trothed to a motley group, ranging from don Pedro Giron (a man of superlative vices), to the Duc d'Berry and Richard III of England. Her arduous trek to the throne, in the menacing shadow of Juana "la Beltraneja," who threatened to displace her, ended on December 13, 1474, when she was proclaimed Queen of Castile.

Ferdinand's dealing with the Cortes of Aragón doubtless contributed to his reputation for high diplomacy and low cunning. Machiavelli observed that Ferdinand had become, with regard to fame and glory, the first King in Christendom.[6] Isabella did not approve of Aragonese ways. She was direct and authoritarian, and found the deviousness of the parliamentary approach intolerable. She was more autocratic, more inclined to severity and less to negotiation, than Ferdinand. Her taste in literature ran to chivalry and religious literature, his to history and music, possessing to an exalted degree that nearly religious sensuality concerning women, gold, and jewels typical of medieval man.[7] The twilight pessimism of the waning Middle Ages was giving way to a guarded optimism and a joyous expectation, blending its dwindling residue with a new extravagant violence.

This oddly matched but complementary couple set the stage on which Spanish life would perform for well over a century. Their influence would outlast the House of Trastamara and continue to exercise its allure even after Spain was delivered into the hands of the House of Hapsburg with its middle European involvements. Their myth endured to recent times when it was resuscitated in the cause of national unity by the Franco regime and still floats uneasily in the Spanish collective unconscious.

There are many conjectures as to who was the majority shareholder in this partnership. Although the consensus tilts towards Isabella, the two were so closely intertwined that both can be held responsible for decisions made and actions taken. However, it should be noted that while Ferdinand chose the jurists, economists and financiers,

6. Niccolò Machiavelli, *The Prince,* trans. Luigi Ricci (New York: Modern Library, 1950), 82.

7. Hillgarth, *op. cit.,* 2:351-52.

Isabella is credited with selecting the three men who most furthered royal interests: Gonzalo de Córdoba (the "Great Captain"), Cardinal Cisneros, and Christopher Columbus. In her case, imagination and instinct prevailed.

Apart from the discovery of the New World and the expulsion of the Jews, the most noteworthy events of their reign were the conquest of Granada and Naples, the reform of the clergy and the establishment of the Inquisition. The war against Granada, the last bastion of Islam in Spain, lasted some nine years. The struggle was both military and political, ranging from the use of heavy artillery *(bombardas)* to political moves made possible by the coercion of the unfortunate *"Rey Chico"* Boabdil.

The strategy employed at Granada was used to great effect in Italy against the French armies and their Swiss auxiliaries, the point of departure for two centuries of Spanish rule. The surrender of Granada, the ancient "city of the Jews" *(Igronatat Al-Yahud),* after an eight-month siege finally put an end to a struggle that lasted for nearly eight hundred years which began in 718 AD when Pelayo was declared King by a group of wild mountaineers in some forgotten niche of Asturias.

*   *   *

The Inquisition is one of those astonishing events that can be explained only by a radical lowering of intellectual tone. Like morganatic marriage, if it didn't exist it would have to be invented. It responded to the times: Medieval *convivencia* (co-existence) had disintegrated. The riots of 1391 created a large group of disgruntled converts (New Christians, *conversos*) who inhabited a no-man's-land between Christianity and Judaism, exacerbating prevailing enmities while at the same time creating new ones. Although Papal inquisitors had been sent at the request of Raymond of Peñafort (+1238), the Inquisition beginning in 1478 dealt with the Albigensian peril and was short lived as the *Siete Partidas* (Legal Code) of Alfonso the Wise gave it its *coup de grâce.*

A fatal conjunction of religious unsettlement, national pride, political strategy, and the promptings of Fray Tomás de Torquemada (+1498) persuaded the monarchs to establish a pristinely Spanish Inquisition. Authorized by a Papal Bull of 1479, it appointed Torquemada (confessor of both monarchs and the nephew of a distinguished Cardinal) as Inquisitor General in 1483. He would hold this post until his death in 1498. Although its long-range effects proved to be pernicious, the Inquisition promised immediate advantages in that it could help to unify the nation, guarantee religious orthodoxy, keep Rome's watchdogs at bay, and stifle opposition among the nobility and clergy.

Its excesses came to be monumental, although these excesses rested more in the mind of its critics than in reality. The estimate of some ten thousand human beings "relaxed" (burnt at the stake) during Torquemada's regency alone, based on the account of Llorente and followed by H. C. Lea, has been drastically revised.[8] Doubtless, the Inquisition proved to be a factor, perhaps the major factor, in the decline of Spain from Imperial grandeur to humiliating obscurity. However, the Inquisition was not without its merits. It recognized the danger presented by the *alumbrados* (Illuminati) before Rome came to recognize it and was responsible for debunking the witchcraft hysteria that later caused such devastation in middle Europe.

The clergy, in a deplorable state when Ferdinand and Isabella ascended to the throne, presented a task of monumental proportions requiring delicate negotiations with an often-vacillating Papacy. The monarchs obtained control of ecclesiastical appointments, and encouraged the Bishops to reside in their dioceses and toe the line theologically and (when necessary) politically. With few exceptions, the reform bishops were reputable and capable, less warlike and more learned than their predecessors. The Council of Seville's 1478 edict against clerical concubinage, absenteeism, simony, and scandal was enforced, albeit selectively. Through diplomacy or more concrete inducements the monarchs gained the support of Pope Alexander VI, Rodrigo Borgia, a brave and prudent man but notorious for his avarice, sensuality, and nepotism — a man who Machiavelli considered that of all the Pontiffs who ever reigned, best showed how a Pope might prevail both by money and by force.[9]

---

8. Refer to Henry Kamen, *The Spanish Inquisition* (New York: Mentor, 1968) *passim*.
9. Machiavelli, *op. cit.,* 43.

Although reform among the secular clergy left much to be desired, it proceeded apace among the religious orders. Several important monasteries were reformed and were then able to serve as models for other religious communities: Guadalupe, Miraflores, Montserrat, and Poblet among them. The Cistercians, Benedictines, and the observant wings of the Franciscans and Dominicans took the lead. When Cardinal Cisneros took charge, the reform made giant strides, due mainly to the impetus provided by this ascetic, energetic, high-minded, violent Friar. A study in paradox, Cisneros sponsored the new University of Alcalá and its polyglot Bible while incinerating thousands of tomes written in Arabic. As Inquisitor General he systematized the procedures of the Inquisition while removing the most blatant abusers, including the sadistic Cordoban Inquisitor, Lucero. The Cardinal has been called the greatest patron of Spanish culture in modern times.[10] During the same period the University of Salamanca led the world in teaching the Copernican system and flourished to the extent that Erasmus declared that the state of the Liberal Arts in Spain could serve as a model to the most cultivated nations of Europe.[11]

Fray Antonio de Marchena of the Franciscan Monastery of La Rábida sponsored Christopher Columbus. Coming from Portugal where his project had been rejected, Columbus met with two vetoes by Spanish Commissions. De Marchena, however, gained the support of Fray Hernando de Talavera, presider of the first Commission, who initiated an upward spiral when the Duke of Medinaceli and other prominent figures added their weight. It was approved. Columbus embarked on Friday, August 4, 1492, the day following the feast of Our Lady of the Angels, patroness of the monastery of La Rábida. Land was sighted over two months later on October 12, 1492, by the lookout of the *Pinta*, Rodrigo de Triana, a *converso*.[12]

Columbus's record with the Caribbean natives was as dismal as

---

10. *Historia*, Tomo 17, 1:274, 2:699f.

11. Cited by Kamen, *The Spanish Inquisition*, 75.

12. Refer to Samuel Eliot Morison, *Admiral of the Ocean Seas: A Life of Christopher Columbus* (Boston: Houghton Mifflin, 1942).

were his administrative skills. Only the natives shipped to Spain were converted to Christianity, possibly because converts could not be sold or enslaved. When later Columbus returned to Spain in shackles only one additional voyage and six years of life remained, enough to partially restore his reputation and confirm his titles. The Admiral of the Ocean Seas died at Valladolid in 1506. His many flaws cannot tarnish the luster of his discoveries, his extraordinary genius as a navigator, and his religious faith, which, though muddied by ambition, would ultimately spread throughout the entire continent.

Columbus was inspired by the messianic enthusiasm coursing through Spain, percolating down from the aristocracy to the masses. A common belief maintained that Isabella was created miraculously for the redemption of the Kingdom. The African conquests in the first decade of the sixteenth century raised expectations that a crusade for the recovery of the Holy Land was in preparation.[13] In spite of the popular notion that Columbus' goal was to reach Cathay, his ultimate goal was the liberation of Jerusalem and the conversion of the world. Salo Baron notes this semi-visionary, semi-realistic outlook on the world, the profound impact of Christian theology and his dependence on the Psalms and Prophets as interpreted by Nicholas of Lyra.[14]

*   *   *

The monarchs were at first more favorable than not to Jews and New Christians, a good number of whom were employed in key positions. The Crown protected several *aljamas* (Jewish ghettoes) from the depredations of aggressive municipalities such as those of Ávila, Medina del Campo, and Cáceres. On September 6, 1477, a directive putting all *aljamas* under royal protection was issued. However, the monarchs' attitude came to suffer a sea change — probably due to popular agitation,

---

13. Hillgarth, *op. cit.*, 2:363-65; *Historia*, 17, 2:713.

14. Salo Wittmayer Baron, *A Social and Religious History of the Jews* (New York: Columbia U. Press, 1968), 13:133-34. Also my own *Reasons for Our Rhymes* (Grand Rapids: Eerdmans, 2001).

the pressures of a turbulent nobility, and the maneuvers of the Inquisition, which exaggerated the *converso* danger, discovering nests of relapsed *conversos* in such elite groups as the Hieronymite Order and the monastery of Guadalupe, one of their favorite shrines. The procedures of the Inquisition, although thorough to an extreme, generated a noxious temper of mind, a public orthodoxy, which developed into a second and more insidious Inquisition.

In 1467 there were nine days of street fighting between old and New Christians. While some *conversos* retained their old religion clandestinely, others became missionaries to their former brethren, still others rabid persecutors. The *Libro del Alborayque* (1488), written by an Inquisitor of some wit, applied the name of Muhammad's steed, neither horse nor mule, to the New Christians.[15] The intolerant spirit, which destroyed medieval *convivencia,* is nicely reflected in the words of Solomon Ibn Verga: "Judaism is no doubt one of the incurable diseases."[16]

The first auto-da-fé of the New Inquisition was celebrated at Seville on February 6, 1487. Diego de Susán, a wealthy merchant, was accused of plotting to massacre Old Christians. This incident had been prefaced by the assassination of the Inquisitor Pedro de Arbués at Saragossa in September 1485. The proverbial (and probably apocryphal) straw came with the charge that a group of Jews and *conversos* had ritually murdered a Christian child. The insults that the conspirators supposedly hurled at the child as representing the infant Jesus were read aloud in the *plaza mayor* of Ávila on November 16, 1491, and possibly repeated in pulpits throughout Spain.[17]

The Edict of Expulsion was not long in coming. It was dated March 31, 1492, and promulgated at the end of April. Bernáldez, scarcely a friend to the Jewish people, provided a heartrending description of the new exodus:[18]

15. Baron, *op. cit.*, 221.

16. Hillgarth, *op. cit.*, 2:449f.

17. Cited by Baron, *op. cit.*, 451. Refer to Benzion Netanyahu, *Don Isaac Abravanel, Statesman and Philosopher* (Philadelphia: Jewish Pub. Society, 1968), 53-60.

18. Baron, *op. cit.*, 82; 348 n. 1.

They went out from the lands of their birth boys and adults, old men and children. . . . They went by the roads and fields with much labor and ill fortune, some collapsing . . . some dying, others giving birth, others falling ill, so that there was no Christian who was not sorry for them . . . the rabbis were encouraging them and making the women and the boys sing and beat drums and tambourines. . . . And so they went out of Castile.

After the expulsion the New Christians continued to play the traditional Jewish role in Spanish society, acting as a bridge between classes and regions. Some *conversos,* surrounded by a menacing society (under the watchful scrutiny of the Inquisition) and debased by the fiction of *limpieza de sangre* (purity of blood), succumbed to self-hatred and despair.

Others became cynical observers of the "great theatre of the world," an attitude which pervades *La Celestina,* the premier Castilian novel written by *converso* Fernando de Rojas. Still others with Jewish connections made significant contributions to Spanish grandeur. Among these were Juan Luis Vives, the great humanist; Diego Laínez, the second general of the Jesuits; St. Teresa of Ávila; Tomás de Torquemada; Fray Luis de León, perhaps the greatest Castilian poet; and King Ferdinand himself. As the Jesuit historian Juan de Mariana declared: "it was a sad state when virtuous men, because of their great achievements, had to undergo hostility, accusations, and injuries from those who should have been their defenders."[19]

*   *   *

Fourteen ninety-two was truly a landmark year. It saw the expulsion of the Jews, the discovery of the New World, and the death of Lorenzo the Magnificent. The reign of the Catholic Kings made possible the Spanish Golden Age. Yet, in spite of their splendid achievements, their reign set in motion a process that led to Spanish decadence. Even during their lives many projects went awry, including the network of mar-

19. Kamen, *op. cit.,* 94.

riage alliances, central to their policy, which expired with the death of the Infante don Juan. Nevertheless, they left the country stronger and with a future of unlimited possibilities.

But they also left it divided and riddled by suspicion. Scarcely any prominent figure, even the most orthodox, was not subjected to the attentions of the Inquisition. St. Ignatius Loyola, St. Teresa, St. John of the Cross, and many others were not exempt. Oscillating between the heroic and the self-serving, the sublime and the mundane, the Catholic Kings ended their days on a sad note. Isabella, stoically bearing great physical and moral pain, died at Medina del Campo on November 26, 1504. Ferdinand, in sharp contrast to his reputation for avarice, died quite poor at the village of Madrigalejo on January 25, 1516, sixty-seven years before the death of St. Teresa and twenty-six years before the birth of Juan de Yepes, the future St. John of the Cross.

*   *   *

When Allison Peers published his *Spanish Mysticism: A Preliminary Study* in 1924 he stated that the purpose of the book was "to give some idea to English-reading people of the wealth of mystical literature which Spain can boast."[20] He was firmly convinced that the Spain of the Golden Age possessed such a wealth of literary treasure as has never been surpassed in Christian Europe. He approves Rawlinson's comparison of the Elizabethan face, that of a man who conquers the world, and the Castilian, the face of a man who storms the heights of heaven. The Spanish mystics believed they were doing just that. Fray Juan de los Ángeles' *Diálogos de la conquista del reino de Dios (Dialogues of the Conquest of the Kingdom of God)* is representative. The good Friar seems to be more familiar with "God's Indies" than with the overseas Empire being rapidly conquered by Spain.

That paradigmatic Spaniard, Marcelino Menéndez y Pelayo, computed the number of works that can be considered mystical, either pub-

---

20. E. Allison Peers, *Spanish Mysticism: A Preliminary Study* (London: Methuen & Co., 1924)

lished or in manuscript, in the neighborhood of three thousand. Authors of these works are counted in the hundreds.[21] Ramon Llull adumbrated this veritable avalanche of mystical literature in the thirteenth century when he spoke of the tree of the philosophy of love. It was advanced in the sixteenth by a group of Franciscan writers, accompanied, more often followed, by members of other Orders. The Franciscan contingent included Bernardino de Laredo, Francisco de Osuna, the author of six "spiritual alphabets," and Pedro de Alcántara, St. Teresa's advisor and confidant.

The most relevant mystical authors among Dominicans and Augustinians were probably Luis de Granada, Pedro Malón de Chaide, Alonso de Orozco, and Luis de León. The last, being the object of his Salamanca colleagues' envy, spent four years imprisoned by the Inquisition with, among others, García de Cisneros, brother of the great Cardinal and reformer of the Benedictine monastery of Montserrat. His *Exercises for the Spiritual Life* doubtless influenced St. Ignatius Loyola in the composition of his *Spiritual Exercises*. Mystical graces were not confined to the clergy; there were also a surprising number of lay people who lived intense spiritual lives.

In the midst of this euphoria arose a new order, the Discalced Carmelites. It was the reform of an ancient Order with a definite contemplative tilt and was the creation of the spirit and energy of one woman, Teresa de Ahumada (St. Teresa), following the impulse of the Spirit. Sebastián de Orozco, writing on true and false prophecy, attributed the rapid spread of the Discalced Carmelites to the sanctity of Teresa.[22] She aspired to return to the original charism of the Carmelites, which she believed had been sadly compromised.

The history of the Carmelites begins with what has been called one of the curiosities of history. It was asserted that Elijah established a community of hermits on Mount Carmel to which the "sons of the

21. Marcelino Menéndez y Pelayo, *Historia de los Heterodoxos Españoles* (Madrid: BAC, 1960).

22. Ronald Cueto, "On the Significance of the Reform of the Religious Orders . . ." in *Teresa de Jesús and Her World,* ed. Margaret A. Rees (Leeds: Trinity and All Souls College, 1981), 19.

prophets" belonged and which existed without break until the Christian era. According to this tradition, members present at Pentecost were converted and proceeded to build a chapel on Mount Carmel in honor of the Blessed Virgin Mary. The Bollandists rejected this account, and the ensuing controversy with the Carmelites led to a settlement in 1698 when silence was imposed on both parties.

The historical odyssey of the Order begins with a Calabrian crusader named Berthold, who, with ten companions, established themselves as hermits near the cave of Elijah on Mount Carmel. The Latin Patriarch of Jerusalem, Albert of Vercelli, approved a Rule comprised of sixteen articles prescribing a purely eremitical way of life: silence, seclusion, and abstinence. Fray Crisógono maintains that the *De Institutione primorum monachorum,* written around 1150, is the "fount" of Carmelite mysticism. It was adopted by St. Cyril of Constantinople, the third Latin General, in his epistle of 1230 as an authorized source of tradition.[23]

About 1240 the hermits immigrated to Cyprus, then to Sicily, France, and England. Due to the new environment the austerities were mitigated in 1247 and the Rule changed from eremitical to cenobitical on the mendicant model. Together with the Franciscans, Dominicans, and Augustinian Hermits they joined the ranks of the mendicant orders and became known as the White Friars. In a Rule approved by Pope Eugenius IV in 1431, further mitigations were mandated because of the troubles of the times.

The reform of St. Teresa sought to return to the primitive life of the Order of the Blessed Virgin, adopting a Rule without mitigation stressing austerity and contemplation along the lines of that predating the settlement of 1247. After years of sickness, suffering, and opposition, this singular nun lived to see the Discalced made into a separate province under the General of the Order (1580) and thirteen years later, in 1593, by Papal act, made an independent Order. On St. Teresa's death, the great Lope de Vega penned an encomium:[24]

23. Crisógono de Jesús Sacramentado, OCD, *La Escuela Mística Carmelitana* (Madrid: Mensajero, 1930), 38ff.

24. Efrén de la Madre de Dios, OCD, *Teresa de Jesús* (Madrid: BAC, 1981), 246.

Con asombro del profundo,
Teresa, ilustre mujer
Nace en Alba para ser
sol de España y luz del mundo.

"Sun of Spain" and "light of the world." Not a negligible tribute!

*   *   *

This, then, is the kaleidoscopic secular and religious world into which John of the Cross was born and through which he passed almost unnoticed. He was not a philosopher, nor a theologian in the professional sense. John was a man of prayer, inebriated by God and to whom everything else, at best, was but crumbs falling from God's table. The intellectual life he experienced at the University of Salamanca provided a terminology and intellectual structure, but made no major impression on him. He kept aloof from the intramural squabbling endemic to academic and religious circles. Recruited by St. Teresa to be one of the first two male Carmelites, he discarded his aspiration to enter the Carthusians and lived a life that was not much different from that of his meager and impoverished youth.

As a youth he was nearly a universal failure. But many of the skills at which he unsuccessfully tried his hand would later serve him well — for example, his impressive sketch of the crucified Christ, which later inspired Dalí's surrealist painting. John was serious and reflective, given to extreme austerity and excruciating penance, exhibiting little of the quick-witted humor and the all-too-human foibles of St. Teresa. He gave the impression of never diverting his gaze from his ultimate goal, teaching how to attain it by word, deed, example, and above all by silence.

These traits made him appear forbidding although his harshness was usually leavened by charity and tempered by prudence. He succeeded in moderating his zeal and curbing his excesses to become a much-prized confessor and advisor, convinced that at the close of life one will be examined in love. However, he fought a losing battle within the Order, upholding the priority of contemplation over the active life. His prayer to be despised and thought little of was granted with a vengeance.

John sought to embrace *"la cruz a secas"* (the cross unadorned) and followed the narrow path. A man of innerness, graced with mystical favors, he, like the first hermits, cultivated solitude. This poet of the "Dark Night" possessed a delicate sensibility, and a rare appreciation of physical nature, which he perceived as diaphanous with the Divine Perfections. His love of solitude grew in tandem with his love of beauty and the intensity of his spiritual life. It is no coincidence that the ecstatic *Llama de Amor Viva* was written and the *Subida* terminated in Granada, at "Los Martires," where he enjoyed a privileged view of the Sierra Nevada. These observations are, at best, simply clues to the personality of the man, poet, mystic, and saint. We shall attempt in the following pages to flesh out each clue through a careful study of the man and his work.

CHAPTER TWO

The Life

¡Castilla varonil, adusta tierra,
Castilla del desdén contra la suerte,
Castilla del dolor y de la guerra,
tierra inmortal, Castilla de la muerte!

ANTONIO MACHADO[1]

It was in strong, melancholy, somber Castile, land of pain, war, and death that Juan de Yepes was born in 1542 at Fontiveros, a town of some five thousand inhabitants. Like his Divine Lord he was born in poverty and squalor. An early biographer, Jerónimo de San José, marks his lifelong love of poverty, how he always opted for a poor and dark cell, how he rejoiced in the poverty of his brother Francisco, despised by the world yet a hidden saint.[2] His father, Gonzalo de Yepes, from a well-to-do family, was ostracized for marrying Catalina Alvarez, a good

1. Antonio Machado, "Orillas del Duero," in *Poesías Completas* (Madrid: Espasa-Calpe, 1963), 83.
2. *Historia de la vida y virtudes del V. P. Fr. Juan de la Cruz* (1641), cited in Federico Ruiz Salvador, OCD, *Introducción a San Juan de la Cruz* (Madrid: BAC, 1968), 17, 21.

and pious woman, but from a lower social class. Because of this, Gonzalo had no choice but to take up his wife's trade: weaving. They labored together until his early death from a devastating illness that took two years to grind him into the grave.

Left with three children, Catalina attempted to enlist the aid of Gonzalo's relatives. Most were obdurate but one, a physician, provided substantial aid, even taking Francisco into his house to have him educated properly. The simple boy soon demurred, and after about a year, returned to Fontiveros and the family trade. In 1548, when Juan was six, the family moved to Arevalo, and later to Medina del Campo. He was, in the words of Father Vincent McNabb, "this undersized, underfed boy, whose craft was to be in practicing and singing Divine Love."[3]

Juan was enrolled at the Colegio de la Doctrina, a day orphanage for poor children, and there was taught elementary subjects and Christian doctrine, and given the opportunity to apprentice in a trade. He tried his hand at carpentry, tailoring, and painting, failing dismally at each. He found his métier in the humble occupations of begging (for the school) and nursing the sick at the Hospital de la Concepción.[4]

He then attended the Colegio de la Compañía, a Jesuit institution, studying grammar, possibly Greek, Latin, and rhetoric. At the age of twenty-one, Juan left the Colegio, refusing the post of chaplain to the Hospital offered by his patron, Don Alonso Álvarez de Toledo, and entered the Carmelite house of Santa Ana, taking the name of Fray Juan de Santo Mathía. There are good reasons to suppose that he received permission to live according to the strict primitive Rule of the Order.[5] The Carmelite Order of Castile was considered to be somewhat relaxed, as it had not endorsed the reforms of General Audet. He aspired to live under a strict Rule and harbored the aspiration of ultimately entering the Carthusian Order.

Fray Juan was then sent to the College of San Andrés at the Uni-

---

3. "The Mysticism of St. John of the Cross," *Blackfriars Reprints* (n.p., n.d.), 3.

4. Crisógono de Jesús Sacramentado, OCD, *Vida y Obras de San Juan de la Cruz Completas* (Madrid: BAC, 1960), 23-29, 34-37.

5. *Op. cit.*, 52.

versity of Salamanca, on the Right Bank of the Ebro River, the intellectual center of the Carmelite Order for the Iberian Peninsula. Appointed Prefect of Studies he was obliged to explain theses, defend them, and reply to objections. In a few short years he found himself vaulted from the humble provincial world of his childhood to the cosmopolitan world of the university. In fact, it was the golden age of Salamanca. It counted nearly seven thousand matriculated students and included many religious institutions, that of the Dominicans alone housing two hundred Friars. San Andrés was one of the smaller religious houses. It had a regime that would today be considered draconian: students were obliged to attend classes, to walk in pairs dressed in white capes, and to exhibit proper composure. Flogging, fasting, house arrest, and expulsion were used to punish disobedience.[6]

Masters also found themselves subject to regulations. Except for the Chairs of Prime, lectures could not exceed an hour. They must be given without notes aided by an *actuante,* who sat in front of the Master's pulpit and read from the text. All classes were in Latin except for those in Music, Astrology, and Grammar. Some leeway was allowed, however. The text could be subjected to criticism, and although the University statutes prescribed the books of Aristotle and the Master of the Sentences (Peter Lombard), illustrious Masters often chose their own texts. For example, Francisco de Vitoria, noted for his fame in International Law, used St. Thomas Aquinas' *Summa Theologiae.*

The only limitation was professedly that of religious orthodoxy. Nevertheless, Chacón, a historian of the University, records that in the decade of 1560-1570 the study of Averroes and Avicenna made great strides. Moreover, Chairs were established for the teaching of the new Nominalistic philosophies, their occupants recruited directly from Paris.[7] The Carmelite Order itself was not without sympathy to theories elaborated by the Islamic philosophers.

The religious establishments usually recommended the authors and texts favored by their respective Orders — Thomas Aquinas at the

6. *Ibid.,* 55-56.
7. *Historia de la Ciudad de Salamanca,* X.20.

Dominican house, Duns Scotus at the Franciscan, and so forth. The Carmelite College of San Andrés prescribed the works of John Baconthorpe and Michael of Bologna. Though the Carmelite theologians did not constitute a school, some areas of agreement can be found in their works. From Gerald to Michael of Bologna, a period straddling about a century, the Order's principal thinkers denied the real distinction between essence and existence, affirmed that the universal is the confused representation of individual things, and maintained individuation through form,[8] giving a definite tilt towards Averroes and Nominalism. Their influence on Fray Juan is doubtful, as is also his often proclaimed Thomism, which has had energetic supporters such as Jacques Maritain.[9]

The cultural milieu of the Age was characterized by the symbiosis of university and cloister. Salamanca, *"Roma la chica,"* aspired to supersede Paris as the theological center of Christendom. Cardinal Ehrle captured this aspiration in dramatic words: "theological science crossed the Pyrenees . . . into faithful Spain, driven by the storms of the Reformation."[10] Fray Juan de Santo Mathia attended the University for about four years, keeping quietly to himself in an environment pulsating with controversy. One of the most acrimonious disputes took place between *escolásticos* and *escrituristas,* the partisans of the medieval theologians and those of the new Scriptural exegesis. It was furthered by attacks on the Vulgate by the Spanish supporters of Erasmus, highlighted by the fracas centered around the person of Fray Luis de León,[11] which succeeded in giving the great poet an extended vacation in the prisons of the Inquisition.

Precise information regarding Fray Juan's studies at Salamanca is lacking. Nevertheless, the University stipulated the *summulas* (elementary logic), major logic, Aristotelian physics, ethics, and politics for the

---

8. Bartolome M. Xiberta, *De scriptoribus scholasticis saeculi XIV ex Ordine Cermelitarum* (Louvain: Biblioth. De la Rev. d'hist. eccles., 1931), 94ff.

9. Jacques Maritain, *The Degrees of Knowledge* (New York: Scribners, 1959), 319ff.

10. F. Ehrle, "Los manuscritos Vaticanos de la Teología Salamantina," *Estudios Salamantinos* 8 (1928): 157.

11. Jean Vilnet, *La Biblia en la Obra de San Juan de la Cruz* (Buenos Aires: Desclée de Brouwer, 1953), 30, 32.

artistas (liberal arts students). The *teólogos* (theology students) were advised to read Thomas Aquinas, probably the *Prima Secundae* of the *Summa Theologiae*, dealing with morals, and the third part dedicated to the Incarnation and the life of Christ.[12] Later studies at San Andrés Cloister School are so nebulous that a distinguished Carmelite scholar has denied their very existence.[13]

We are on more solid ground regarding his sources and other influences in his works. His preferences run to St. Augustine (usually the *Soliloquia* of the Pseudo-Augustine), Aristotle (cited secondhand), Thomas Aquinas, the Pseudo-Denis, and Pope St. Gregory, none of whom is cited more than six times. Bonaventure and Boethius are cited twice, John Cassian once.[14] However, *los filósofos,* by which the dicta of the Schoolmen are meant, are cited no less than nineteen times. This runs the gamut from the *tabula rasa* theory of cognition to the impossibility of two contraries co-existing in one subject, both of which have a prominent place in his thought.

Other influences can be discerned: the Rhenish mystics such as Ruysbroek and Tauler, the Neoplatonic tradition emanating from Plotinus, perhaps Bonaventure and the Victorines. Fray Basilio Ponce de León, nephew of Fray Luis, used the works of the Victorines to defend Fray Juan when his works were under investigation by the Inquisition. Urs von Balthasar correctly points to the Eastern flavor of Fray Juan's thought, indicating that "many of St. John's *dicta,* if translated into Greek, could be incorporated directly into the *Gnostic Centuries* of Evagrius."[15] This may be something of an exaggeration but hardly out of the question given Fray Juan's predilection for the Pseudo-Denis.

---

12. Bruno de Jesús-Marie, OCD, *St. John of the Cross,* ed. Benedict Zimmerman, OCD (New York: Sheed & Ward, 1932), 15, 36-38.

13. Silverio de Sta. Teresa, OCD, *Historia del Carmen Descalzo* (Burgos: Editorial Burgalesa, 1936), 5:43.

14. E. W. Trueman Dicken, *The Crucible of Love* (London: Darton, Longman & Todd, 1963), 300-301.

15. Hans Urs von Balthasar, *The Glory of the Lord: A Theological Aesthetics,* trans. A. Louth, J. Saward, A. Simon, and R. Williams, ed. John Richer, 3 vols. (San Francisco: Ignatius Press, 1986), 3:131 n. 168.

The one undoubted influence was Scripture. His immediate dependence was immense. Vilnet indicates that in Fray Juan's four major works there are no less than 1,160 Scriptural citations (Old Testament — 684; New Testament — 476). In the Old Testament his preference ran to Job, Jeremiah, and David, men who had experienced periods of great desolation only to be rewarded by God with a special kind of friendship.[16] His favorite New Testament text is the hymn of John 17. Taking each influence into account and balancing it with the others, we may conclude that Fray Juan's thought is the product of a convergence of disparate influences subordinated to a will fixed on the goal of perfection in this life and the possession of God in the next.

*   *   *

We know little of Fray Juan's life as a student. His reputation for extreme austerity and seriousness made him unpopular with his fellow students. (To some he became an object of fear.) He was present when the reform-minded General of the Order, Fray Rubeo, visited Salamanca.

On April 12, 1567, Fray Juan visited Mother Teresa's convent of San José in Ávila, her first foundation. Although she was more than twice his age (fifty-two to twenty-five) the young friar made enough of an impression to be invited to see her again, this time at Medina del Campo, where she was engaged in negotiating the second foundation. Fray Bruno described him in the following terms:[17]

> John was short, about five feet two . . . an air of reflection . . . face oval in shape . . . brown complexion . . . dark eyes . . . a broad high forehead, well marked eyebrows and an almost aquiline nose . . . an impression of peace and nobility like some of Zurbaran's portraits of Carthusian monks.

16. Vilnet, *op. cit.*
17. Bruno, *op. cit.*, 9.

It was a momentous meeting not only for the participants, but also for the Carmelite Order and the history of spirituality. She ended their meeting by recruiting him as one of the first two Discalced Carmelites of the male branch and soon disabused him of his Carthusian aspirations.

Mother Teresa must have overwhelmed him, an entrance into another world. Not only her life but that of her family was an ongoing drama. Don Juan Sanchez, her paternal grandfather, penanced for "judaizing" by the Inquisition, moved from Toledo to Ávila and set up a prosperous business in cloth. This allowed his children not only to make advantageous marriages,[18] but also to receive a patent of nobility. From early childhood Teresa was pious, aspiring to be with God, who alone could give meaning to the word *siempre* (always). Later, she survived an illness that took her to the border of the grave and kept her paralyzed for three years.

After returning to the convent of Concepción Teresa was shocked out of a routine religious life by a vision, the first of a lengthy parade. Her post-conversion life became a dialogue with God in which bits and pieces of the conversation filtered into the everyday world. Together with the burgeoning of her inner life her active life took an energetic turn that led to the foundation of seventeen Discalced convents and the composition of several works of great merit such as the *Vida*, the *Camino de Perfección*, and the *Moradas*. While she was searching for this road to spiritual perfection, her brothers and cousins were engaged in more worldly pursuits, crossing the seas to join the ranks of the conquistadors looking for the road to El Dorado. What most impresses contemporary readers is her courage and high resolve. Very few nuns of any period could have threatened a randy nobleman with decapitation or have had the temerity to visit Cardinal Quiroga, the Grand Inquisitor, when their writing was undergoing scrutiny and walk away with a favorable judgment.[19]

<hr>

18. Efrén de la Madre de Dios, OCD, *Teresa de Jesús* (Madrid: BAC, 1981), 3-6. For a more detailed study, Efrén and Otger Steggink, *Tiempo y Vida de Sta. Teresa* (Madrid: BAC, 1968).

19. *Ibid.*, 208ff.

(If Mother Teresa was unsettling to the sixteenth century, she was no less so to the twentieth. The physician-psychologist Josef Breuer, protesting Janet's negative evaluation of hysterics, enthroned Teresa as "the patron saint of hysterics," observing that "she was a woman of genius and great practical capacity," which demonstrated that "people of intellect, will, character, and the highest critical genius may be found among hysterics."[20] Whatever one may think of this diagnosis by a former associate of Sigmund Freud, the hysteric as a character type is, in many ways, preferable to other types such as the phobic and the obsessive-compulsive.)

Fray Juan was a serious, reflective man with little of Mother Teresa's quick humor or charm. He gives the impression of never unfixing his gaze from the ultimate goal. He teaches constantly: by word, deed, example, and above all, by silence. In 1568 Mother Teresa had accepted a small house (hovel would be closer to the truth) at Duruelo, some nine leagues from Ávila. The first male Discalced community was established there. Fray Juan and a lay brother, later joined by Fray Antonio de Heredia (even later by his mother and brother Francisco) toiled to adorn the house with pious sketches, crosses, and skulls. The act of foundation took place on November 28, 1568. Fray Juan signed his name *Juan de la Cruz,* the name he bore thereafter. The community moved to Mancera seven months later, with a roster of well over fifteen religious.[21]

A visit to the Prince of Eboli led to his appointment as Rector of the Discalced house at the University of Alcalá, the recent creation of Cardinal Jiménez. After a brief tenure, Mother Teresa requisitioned him as confessor to the troubled nuns of the Encarnación, to which she had been grudgingly returned as Prioress. A combination of substantial donations and able work in the confessional remedied the situation. In the face of his reputation as severe and intransigent, Fray Juan advised a

---

20. Josef Breuer and Sigmund Freud, *Studies on Histeria,* standard edition, *The Complete Works of Sigmund Freud,* ed. James Strachey (London: The Hogarth Press, 1971), I:232.

21. Crisógono, *op. cit.,* 77; 83-85.

timid young penitent that "the more holy the confessor, the less he is scandalized by others' faults, and the less harsh he is."[22]

The *Instruction to Discalced Novices*, which he possibly helped formulate, is a clue to his spirituality: "Notice especially that we should not go to our prayers to find ourselves but to flee from ourselves."[23] This forgetfulness of self, coupled with his love of silence and abhorrence of the crowd and its mentality, is the point of departure for unrelenting reductionism that clears away everything that stands in the way of the ultimate goal. Yet, Fray Juan was not, as the poet Jorge Guillén believed, totally withdrawn from the world, living as in a desert.[24] Albeit a friend of recollection and silence, his evangelizing works, as well as his many tasks and obligations, took him into the world. In the troubles approaching on the horizon the world was all too much with him.

The Carmelites of the Ancient Observance — the Calced — quickly became disenchanted with the Teresian Reform. Its success brought a number of unstable characters into the fold. To the grotesque antics of these new recruits was added the belief that the very existence of the Order was threatened. Strong measures were adopted at the General Chapter of Piacenza (May 1575) and a Visitor General, Fray Jerónimo Tostado, was sent to Spain to implement its decisions. Mother Teresa was put under house detention and several Discalced, Fray Juan included, were arrested. He was imprisoned in the large Carmelite house in the Imperial City of Toledo, where he was beaten regularly, starved, and locked in a dark, narrow, asphyxiating cubicle. Once used as a privy, it lacked even a small window.[25]

After six months of this harsh treatment, a more compassionate jailer was assigned. John was given a clean tunic and, more importantly, pen and paper. Despite these appalling conditions, he composed *liras* (lyric poems) and *romances* (epic poems) as well as the greater parts of the *Cántico Espiritual* (Spiritual Canticle) and the *Noche Oscura* (Dark Night),

22. *Ibid.*, 112.
23. Cited by Trueman Dicken, *op. cit.*, 213.
24. Jorge Guillén, *Lenguaje y poesía* (Madrid: Revista de Occidente, 1962), 102.
25. Crisógono, *op. cit.*, 124-35; 143-45.

in which images of darkness, pain, depression, and sorrow accompany the pervading symbolism of night. Jean Baruzi claims that the symbolism of "dark night" springs from his most elevated and inward reality.[26]

Night runs through Fray Juan's life as it does his poetry. He was taken prisoner on the night of December 2, 1577 and escaped on the night of August 14, 1578. Recovering somewhat, he was present at the Discalced Chapter of Almodóvar (October 9, 1578), at which he was appointed Superior of the small house of El Calvario and confessor to the nuns at Beas. At Beas he had an encounter that greatly impressed Roy Campbell, a gifted translator of his verse:[27]

> One day he asked a nun in what her prayer consisted . . . [it consisted] in considering the beauty of God and rejoicing that he has such beauty . . . the saint was so pleased with this that for some days he said the most sublime things concerning the beauty of God at which he marveled.

This account is a good illustration of what Urs von Balthasar rather pedantically calls "aesthetic theology," which stands in sharp opposition to the Reformational spirit of banning aesthetics from theology. If beauty was, as he urges, an obsession[28] for Fray Juan, it was one that was accompanied by spiritual charisms and charity towards others. He remained rigorously austere: His cell at the Calvario contained only a cross, an image of the Virgin, a skull, a discipline (whip), and one or two books.

He was given the task of founding the first Discalced College in Andalusia at Baeza, a prosperous town of about fifty thousand with a small but flourishing university. There he attended to his academic duties while ministering to the sick and dedicating himself to spiritual direction.[29] As if by reward to his struggle, a favorable decision to the

26. Cited by Urs von Balthasar, *op. cit.*, 3:125.

27. Roy Campbell, *The Poems of St. John of the Cross*, preface by M. C. D'Arcy, SJ (London: Harvill, 1953); Crisógono, *op. cit.*, 182.

28. Urs von Balthasar, *op. cit.*, 3:125.

29. Crisógono, *op. cit.*, 196-98; 202-3.

Carmelite intramural struggle was issued by Pope Gregory XIII. On June 22, 1580, the Pope issued a brief separating the Discalced from the Calced. At the Chapter of Almodóvar (May 1, 1583) Fray Jerónimo Gracián was elected provincial. He proceeded to lock horns with Fray Juan over the issue of missionary activity: Gracián favored it; Juan did not, arguing that it contradicted the contemplative charism of the Order. Juan was posted to Granada as Provincial Vicar — a move that was both unwelcome and fortuitous.

The Carmelite house was located on the hill of Anabul, enjoying a privileged view of the Sierra Nevada. Fray Juan must have reveled in the sight of glorious flowers, mountains, and stars. Love of natural beauty grew parallel to his love of solitude. In his writings nature becomes diaphanous, a veil through which the Divine Attributes are faintly discerned. His aspiration for God prods him to such an extreme that Baruzi can speak of a 'cosmic ecstacy.'[30] This is not a radical turn to a world that he had left behind, a frank denial of his contemplative vocation. Quite the opposite, it is precisely because of his fidelity to the contemplative vocation that the external world becomes no more than a fragile mask: "no more than the husk or shell of reality which prevents us from apprehending reality itself."[31]

Together with his quest for solitude and more intense appreciation of nature, his generosity expanded prodigally and his mystical gifts flourished. He would take his Friars into the countryside and have each find a solitary place in which to meditate. He was at times seen rapping his knuckles on the house wall attempting to disengage himself from the things of God.[32] To the question "What is God?" a simple lay brother (Fray Francisco) gave an answer which Fray Juan applauded: "*Dios es lo que él se quiere,*"[33] which can loosely translated as "God is what He wishes to be." This is astonishingly similar to the literal trans-

---

30. Jean Baruzi, *Saint Jean de la Croix et le problème de l'expérience mystique* (Paris: Alcan, 1924), 278-81.

31. *Subida*, II.17.6.

32. Crisógono, *op. cit.*, 321.

33. Cited in Crisógono, *op. cit.*, 350.

lation of God's enigmatic answer to Moses: *"Ehyeh esher ehyeh"* (I will be who I will be).

These vignettes provide a fragmentary picture of a life of piety characterized by intense devotion to the Trinity, an inner life that often erupted into his everyday life. The aftereffects of a spiritual experience might last for an entire day. Yet his productivity increased. The *Cántico* was completed, as was the *Subida* (Ascent to Mount Carmel). Prodded by Mother Ana de Jesús, he composed his ecstatic *Llama de Amor Viva* (Flame of Living Love) in fifteen days.[34] There are reports that he wrote a work entitled *Propiedades del Pájaro Solitario* (Properties of the Solitary Songbird), which, unfortunately, has been lost. It is possible that other works, written or in progress, were destroyed, the casualties of persecution that would mark his last days.

Fray Juan de la Cruz was caught between Fray Nicolás Doria, an ascetic, hard-nosed bureaucrat, and Fray Jerónimo Gracián, a charming but naïve man of affairs. Doria appreciated Juan's gifts, but only to the extent that he, Doria, could make use of them. Gracián, who was defended by Fray Juan, did not have one gesture of defense or one word of praise for him in his writings.[35] Mother Teresa had died in 1583 and even she, who interceded with Philip II in favor of Fray Juan, favored Gracián. Perusing Gracián's *Peregrinación de Anastasio,* an account of his adventures, we find an interesting but superficial personality favored by bizarre visions of geometric complexity. Between Doria, who considered Juan a piece on the chessboard and Gracián, who thought of him as a cipher, a non-person, there was little hope for the poor friar.

Fray Juan opposed Doria on three principal matters: his persecution of Gracián (which ultimately succeeded), his projected changes in the Carmelite Rule, and his projected separation of the nuns from the male province, *viz.,* their virtual expulsion.[36] Doria was not a man to take opposition kindly. Fray Juan was dismissed from his posts, returned to Andalusia, and named to head a Carmelite missionary expe-

34. *Ibid.,* 321.
35. Ruiz Salvador, *op. cit.,* 61.
36. Trueman Dicken, *op. cit.,* 23, 26, 27.

dition to Mexico. However, Fray Juan received the news calmly. During this period he wrote to Mother María de la Encarnación at Segovia (July 6, 1591):[37]

> God orders everything . . . and where there is no love put love and you shall draw out love.

Fray Diego Evangelista, empowered by the Consulta (the ruling body set up by Doria) to complete the investigation of Gracián, included Fray Juan, probably intending to penalize both with expulsion. He did not balk at insulting his witnesses, extorting, and falsifying testimonies. Fray Juan was now living at La Peñuela, a small house lost in the Sierra Morena, a half league or so from the Navas de Tolosa, where, in 1212 the Almohades received a great defeat that laid Islamic Spain at the feet of Christian Spain. There, Fray Juan led his usual ascetic life dedicated to contemplation.

Falling victim to recurrent illness and general weakness, the result of ill treatment and severe self-discipline, he went to the Carmelite house at Úbeda, ostensibly to undergo a cure. A prior still resentful from a reprimand he received from Fray Juan years ago assigned him the poorest and smallest cell. As if that were not enough, the dying friar was obliged to join in community activities and found food and medicine in short supply.

Fray Juan was also subjected to hideous cures that generated great welts, tumors, and vast amounts of pus.[38] He was barely able to speak but recited passages from Scripture and repeated short prayers. Baruzi maintains that in his reaction to the ongoing persecution, Fray Juan "attains a grandeur that we can say is unique in the history of Christian spirituality."[39] Juan embraced *la cruz a secas* (the cross unadorned), which he had pursued so ardently since his youth.

On his deathbed Fray Juan instructed his nurse for more patience,

---

37. Cited by Crisógono, *op. cit.*, 350.
38. *Ibid.*, 369, 379-80.
39. Baruzi, *op. cit.*, 218-19.

more love, and more pain.[40] His extravagant sensibility reemerged at the last moment. He asked that verses from the Song of Songs be read. "Qué preciosas margaritas," he murmured, then expired. Eyewitnesses report that his face became white, transparent, and luminous, with the fragrance of roses emanating from his devastated body.[41] Whether the simple truth or merely religious imagination run amok, it is a most beautiful tribute.

Pope Clement X beatified Fray Juan de la Cruz on January 25, 1675. Benedict XIII canonized him on December 26, 1726, and Pius XI solemnly declared him Doctor of the Universal Church on August 24, 1926.

Perhaps the most fitting tribute, aside from the ecclesiastical pronouncements, was given by Discalced Carmelite and martyr, Edith Stein:[42]

> We can only thank him that he has allowed us a glance at a marvelous country, an earthly paradise on the threshold of the heavenly one.

40. Crisógono, *op. cit.*, 380.

41. *Ibid.*, 384-386.

42. Edith Stein, *The Science of the Cross,* trans. Hilda Graef (Chicago: Henry Regnery, 1960), 164.

CHAPTER THREE

Mapa Mundi

Here is a Dante deprived of all images and concentrated in a single interior experience. Instead of
ditches, cornices and spheres, there is nothing except
God.

HANS URS VON BALTHASAR[1]

Neither the person nor the works of St. John of the Cross appeal to
a contemporary audience. This age of the chattering mass can
but little sympathize with a man of silence, recollection, and self-
discernment. Even the reader with religious sympathies who may have
a passing admiration for his verse stops short of the commentaries,
which tend toward the dry and repetitive. St. John indicates that those
experiences that arise from mystical understanding are not fully expli-
cable.[2] The poem is the bridge between the experience and its formula-

---

1. Hans Urs von Balthasar, *The Glory of the Lord: A Theological Aesthetics*, trans.
A. Louth, J. Saward, M. Simon, and R. Williams, ed. John Richer, 3 vols. (San Francisco:
Ignatius Press, 1986), 3:112.

2. *Cántico*, prol.

tion in discursive language. It is impregnated by an élan that extends the range and enriches the possibilities of language.

The mystical event is first crystallized into verse before it is formulated in the shape of a commentary that can be said to decode it. This latter scarcely possesses the beauty and force of the poem and marks a move downward. Yet it is the commentary[3] that we are obliged to deal with when we attempt to decipher St. John's thought. The three commentaries provide us with an entrance into an alien world. Nonetheless, within this welter of psychological descriptions, ascetic methodology, spiritual counsel, and anecdote, it is possible to discern a phenomenology of the spirit as well as an inchoate philosophy of humanity, creation, and God, all under guidance of a ruthless logic.

St. John is single-minded, everything concentrated in an incandescent point. St. Augustine cries: "Oh, Lord, I love you. I burn, I pant for you. I trample underfoot all that gives here delight. I want to go to you."[4] This is assuredly the leitmotiv of his thought but hardly the sole refrain. In the case of St. John of the Cross, the pursuit of God is the entire symphony, the sole object of an indomitable will fixated on the one true reality. It operates within a scheme of opposites. On the one pole creatures, on the other the Creator, on the one Nothing, on the other the All: night at an infinite distance from flame.

For many years the Carmelite desert of Our Lady of the Snows in Málaga venerated an autograph copy of a drawing of the mystical Mount Carmel by Fray Juan de la Cruz. It was probably modeled on the famous *tabula cebetica* of the University of Salamanca.[5] The most noteworthy aspect of the sketch is the path that climbs directly to the summit of the mount. This is "the path of the spirit of perfection." On it

3. There are three commentaries: to the *Cántico,* to the *Llama,* and to the *Subida Noche.* As the *Noche* was originally the fourth book of the *Subida,* it should be regarded as a single commentary.

4. *Sermo* 159.8.

5. Michel Florisone, "Esthétique et Mystique d'après Sainte Thérèse de Avila et Saint Jean de la Croix," in *La Vigne du Carmel* (Paris: Ed. Du Seuil, 1956), 117-21. Several reproductions are given in Crisógono, *op. cit.,* 408-12.

the following words are inscribed: *NADA, NADA, NADA, NADA,* and even on the mount, *NADA.* Why this glut of nothings?

At first sight this "path of nothings" seems to be perilously close to nihilism. Some have thought so. Dom John Chapman, for example, disliked the saint for fifteen years, calling him a Buddhist. He quoted the view of an unnamed Abbot that St. John is like a sponge full of Christianity: you squeeze it all out and the full mystical theory re - mains.[6] This is a common misconception. The path of nothings is ensconced within Christian asceticism. It portrays the necessary voiding or stripping of the soul and its powers of intellect, memory, and will to arrive at union with God. The nothings are not ends in themselves but the means to arrive at the TODO, the ALL, God.

The texts which Karol Wojtyla (Pope John Paul II) indicates are key to his study of faith in the works of St. John of the Cross[7] (an interesting study possibly influenced by the singular Thomism of his mentor, Father Garrigou-Lagrange) are pertinent. In brief, these texts indicate that creatures cannot serve as the proximate and proportionate means for union with God. The only means, the only avenue to God, is faith. As God does not fall under genera or species he transcends the powers of the human mind. He is transcendent in the most rigorous sense.

Faced with the problem of God's transcendence St. Thomas Aquinas tilted towards the *via remotionis.* It is possible to arrive at a certain though partial knowledge of the unknowable Deity by knowing what He is not. However, he did place apophatic theology in its highest form at the pinnacle of meditation on God and Being. As Gilson suggests, perhaps anguish in the face of pure being is nothing more than another name for the fear of God.[8] What St. Thomas views as the apex of the spiritual life, St. John accepts as a unique vocation, the *way of unknowing.*

6. Cited by T. Dicken, *op. cit.,* 325.

7. Karol Wojtyla (Pope John Paul II), *Faith According to St. John of the Cross,* trans. Alvaro Huerga (Madrid: BAC, 1979), 16, 25. The texts are *Subida,* II.8-9.

8. *Summa Contra Gentiles,* I.14.2; I.21.2; I.28.2; Étienne Gilson, *L'Être et l'Essence* (Paris: Via, 1948), 28ff.

The quest for union with God does not rest satisfied with fragmentary knowledge dredged up by the intellect. *A posteriori* reasoning begins with creatures, which, in St. John's view, are "like crumbs that have fallen from God's table."[9] To gorge on them after the manner of beasts would impede the soul from rising from these "crumbs" to the Uncreated Spirit of the Father. Expanding the formula of Lateran Council IV, he affirms that the difference between Creator and creature is infinite; creatures, at best, can serve only to whet the appetite.[10]

St. John recurs to a "rule of philosophy" that means must be proportioned to their ends. As we have noted, this is not the case of creatures *vis-à-vis* God who is "of another being than His creatures and infinitely distant from them."[11] The consideration of creatures can provide only vague intimations of their Creator, "stammerings" that serve only to intensify the suffering of the soul approaching God. Doubtless, creatures do represent something of what God is, but they should not be made the object of our complete attention.

The *De Institutione Primorum Monachorum,* of such importance to the Carmelite Order, indicates that if a being descends to a level lower than itself, it "mixes" on this level and suffers a proportionate degradation.[12] This is perhaps an application of the Gospel's maxim, "Where your treasure is, there will your heart be also" (Matthew 6:21 NRSV). St. John takes up the principle: the soul falls to the level of the creature it desires, *"se iguala,"* becomes equal to it, as "love effects a likeness between the lover and the object loved."[13] The ancient Platonic chestnut is situated in a new and novel context.

While the *Subida* is relatively sober, at times appealing to scholastic dicta, the *Cántico,* florid and Scriptural, paints a more attractive but no less negative picture of creatures. In the strophe *pasó por estos sotos con presura* he lauds the graces that God has poured out on creatures — *"mil gracias,"* a thousand graces! They are doubly indebted to their Cre-

9. *Subida,* I.6.3.

10. *Denziger,* 432. Cited by Wojtyla, *op. cit.,* 27. *Subida,* II.8.3.

11. *Subida,* III.12.1.

12. *De Institutione Primorum Monachorum,* VI.52.

13. *Subida,* I.4.2.

ator — both because of their creation *ex nihilo* and because of the Incarnation, which effects a second creation superior to the first, "clothing" creatures completely in beauty.[14] This was later repeated by Bérulle in his *De la double création de l'homme*. By the first creation we are God's servants; by the second, His children.[15]

Nonetheless, the beauty and grandeur of creation is nothing compared to its Divine Source. They, at most, are very dim reflections of the Divine Attributes, those "lamps of fire" which are "living waters of the spirit."[16] Still, in a move reminiscent of the Pythagoreans, St. John maintains that creatures combined give voice to a symphony that is superior to all the worldly harmonies when each creature gives voice to what God is in it. Yet creatures do not carry their own justification but point to the Invisible Beauty — their "root and life," who created them.[17] For if humankind were to be imbedded in the world of creatures without hope of transcending it,

> We would live on in twilight,
> Our life devoid of meaning . . .

This in a sense assuredly not meant by Hofmannsthal!

The soul cannot remain static. It must either ascend to God or descend to creatures. It lives in an uncomfortable halfway house. This is explained in the *Subida* employing a scholastic principle again culled from the Platonic tradition:[18]

> As we learn in philosophy . . . two contraries cannot co-exist in the same subject. Darkness, an attachment to creatures, and light, which is God, are contraries and have no likeness to each other.

14. *Cántico*, V.4.

15. Cited by Henri de Lubac, *The Mystery of the Supernatural*, trans. Rosemary Sheed (New York: Sheed & Ward, 1967), 119-20.

16. *Llama*, III.8.

17. *Cántico*, XXXIX.11; XIV-XV.25; VI.1.

18. *Subida*, III.12.2.

It follows that the soul desiring spiritual perfection must discard its attachment to creatures so as to dispose itself for the reception of God. Light will enter the soul only if the contrary form, the darkness of creatures, is ejected. This is accomplished by means of detachment. In a text that seems to border on the presumptuous, St. John suggests that when the soul disengages itself from things and attains emptiness regarding them, God will not fail to do His part by communicating Himself, "at least silently and secretly."[19]

St. Paul's distinction between the Old and the New Self is appropriated to describe the movement from darkness to light. The former, St. John indicates, is completely absorbed by the world, the "animal man" who lives by appetite and suffers from *"embotamiento de la mente,"* a blunting of the mind. And for the new to live, the old must die. The process by which this transition takes place is a cleansing or purgation, often called a *"desnudar,"* a stripping or divesting:[20]

> God makes the soul die to all that He is not so that when it is stripped and flayed of its old skin, He may clothe it anew.

Its youth is then renewed, like the eagle's (Isaiah 40:31), and the soul becomes new, created according to God. Rising above the self to a supernatural dimension, the individual becomes a child of God above anything that can be thought.

This transition is an arduous and, from what St. John tells us, a painful journey. It is not accomplished by a Kierkegaardian leap but through many "preparatory acts" connected in an orderly fashion in which each act is the preparation and foundation for the next. It first purifies the external part of the self, then the internal. This is the work of the "nights," of which there are two: the active nights of sense and spirit of voluntary self-discipline; the passive nights in which God Himself works on the soul. Both nights have two phases, one that affects the senses, and a second that affects the spirit in its three "faculties" of understanding, memory, and will.

19. *Subida*, I.4.3.
20. *Noche*, II.13.11; *Llama*, II.33.

The active nights cleanse by means of all the tools of asceticism from prayer to corporeal penance. They bring about detachment from things (Night of Sense) and the purging of the soul's imperfections (Night of the Spirit). But only when it enters into the passive night does the soul become contemplative and enter the path to the state of the "perfect" — the union of the soul with God.[21] St. John depicts the passive nights in frightening terms. They reach their summit in the Passive Night of the Spirit.[22] This crucible is so dreadful that many souls become unsettled and turn back. This is hardly a doctrine for the fainthearted.

This ascent is not self-propelled nor does it take place solely within the confines of the soul. St. John uses a metaphor previously employed by Plotinus and the Pseudo-Denis,[23] the sculpting of a statue:[24]

> Not everyone capable of hewing the wood knows how to carve the statue, nor does everyone able to carve know how to polish it, nor do all who know how to polish know how to paint it, nor do all of these know how to perfect it and bring the work to completion.

To "hew" is to guide the soul to contempt of the world, the *mundus;* to "carve" is to introduce the soul to holy meditation, and so forth, to represent the various stages in the soul's ascent to God. The entire fabric of religious life requires the assistance of experienced directors to hone the soul to the point that God brings it to completion.

The torments of the passive night are almost as interesting to psychopathology as to spirituality. The purgation of the appetites causes the natural self to apparently wilt, to dry up. One undergoes a metamorphosis of the self, a radical change both physically and psychologically agonizing. The person changes, loses the foothold possessed as a definite self, and does not know what changes are in the offing.

21. *Subida,* I.2.5; *Noche,* I.1.1.
22. *Noche,* I.8.2.
23. *Enneads,* I.6.9; *De Mystica Theologie,* 2.
24. *Llama,* III.57ff.

However, at the end of the process when the soul is emptied of "the juices of sense," it is possible to begin to experience infused contemplation.[25] Furthermore, when the "roots" and "traces" of the capital sins have been excised from the soul, it arrives at the freedom of spirit and is liberated from its three principal enemies: the world, the flesh, and the Devil.

The soul must pass through the portal of this (passive) night of the spirit to arrive at union with God. This is the highest mode, as He dwells substantially in all created things and, more specifically, in the human soul through grace. However, when God teaches the soul secretly, instructing it in the perfection of love, it disposes the soul for transforming, divinizing union. The negative side resides in the pain and torment caused by the Divine Wisdom it receives, a corollary of the radical disparity between God's transcendence and the human soul's low estate. Union in this life is both an anticipation of heaven and a foretaste of purgatory as it bestows the same "fire of loving wisdom" that illuminates the angels in heaven.[26]

At this point contemporary readers, unaccustomed to delve into these thickets, will stop to reflect. Much will have struck them as odd and bizarre. Aside from their unfamiliarity with the subject, the endemic weakness of language takes its toll. God may be near to our being, but He is far from our thinking. Religious language has its peculiarities. On the highest level it would seem that the immense flow of words by which humankind praises God should be reciprocated by a superior flow from God. Yet, St. John tells us that God, in giving us His Son, spoke everything in one Word, "and He has no more to say."[27] This ascent from darkness to light, from multiplicity to unity, need not be expressed in unfamiliar terms. St. Augustine can caution his parishioners in plain language:[28]

---

25. *Noche*, I.12II.
26. *Noche*, II.5.1-2.
27. *Subida*, II.22.3.
28. *Sermo* 169.18.

On earth we are wayfarers, always on the go. This means we have to keep moving forward. Therefore, be always unhappy about what you are if you want to reach what you are not.

But his language necessarily becomes more dense and technical when penning a theological treatise or a letter to a cultivated friend.

For St. John there is only one "ladder" that reaches from the individual to God — the "secret ladder" that is faith. This is why we rise by *unknowing* rather than by knowing, "by the soul blinding itself and remaining in darkness rather than by opening its eyes."[29] This notion is reiterated in the *Cántico* through the metaphor of the *"cristalina fuente"* (crystalline spring). Faith is crystalline in that it is pure and cleansed of error, and a spring because from it all spiritual goods flow; the metaphor has possible roots in the descriptions of Eternal Wisdom found in Ecclesiasticus (24:5ff.). The articles of faith are described as the "silver surface" of the spring, as they present God to us covered with the silver of faith.[30]

A similar metaphor is used in a poem St. John wrote while imprisoned at Toledo, *"Cantar del alma que se huelga de conocer a Dios por fe."* The *"fonte"* in the poem signifies the spring of living water, the Word of God received by faith. Fr. David Rubio notes the distinction between *saber* and *conocer* in Spanish. The first signifies knowing by means of intuition; the second, knowing through the exercise of reason. This corresponds to the scholastic distinction between *ratio* and *intellectus,* the power of discursive thought and simple vision. The strophe which begins *"Qué bien sé yo la fonte que mana y corre"* signifies that the purity of faith cannot be attained by means of discursive reason but by intuition which voids the understanding of every item of discourse and reasoning.[31]

This is reminiscent of the transition from *dianoia* (discursive rea-

29. *Subida,* II.8.5.
30. *Cántico,* XII.3; XII.4.
31. David Rubio, OSA, *La "fonte" de San Juan de la Cruz* (La Habana: Minerva, 1946), 12-15.

son) to *noesis* (insight) in Plato's *Republic* as well as the elevation to the One in Plotinus' *Enneads*.[32] However, in both the Platonic ascent to the Idea of the Good and the Plotinian to the One there is more than an element of autocratic self-satisfaction which is absent in St. John of the Cross. The distinction between the Platonic lover of wisdom and the Sanjuanist contemplative is that between self-affirmation and docility, activity and letting oneself be acted upon.

Mystical contemplation, then, is a knowing but not a knowing born of discursive reason. It is a knowledge through love, an infused knowledge placed by God directly in the (passive) intellect.[33] It bypasses the natural cognitive apparatus that has its obligatory point of departure in sensation. Although St. John endorses the Aristotelian maxim that nothing reaches the intellect without first passing through the senses, this applies to natural reason. In mystical contemplation God infuses knowledge quietly and secretly in darkness to material things.

When we speak of knowledge through love it must be emphasized that this is not love as understood by sentimentalists or by the pious advocates of the maudlin attitudes castigated by St. John. Even the Renaissance scholar and translator of his verse, Arthur Symonds, was somewhat off the mark when he exclaimed, "this monk can give a lesson to lovers."[34] Love must be elevated to a spiritual level. A pertinent example is that of Mother Ana de Jesús, who would give strophes of the *Cántico* to novices from a worldly background and lead them from the carnal interpretation to the spiritual while marking their progress. Love gives the soul that ultimate substantial openness that is beyond pleasure and pain.

In the *Cántico,* a poem written in the "burning love" of God, the soul initially views God as far distant, hidden. Attempts to contact Him directly are unsuccessful. The soul then turns to intermediaries implor-

32. Plato *Republic* 506bf; Plotinus *Enneads* VI.8-9.

33. Scholastic epistemology, inspired by Aristotle, taught there were two parts, or aspects, to the human intellect: the passive, in which knowledge resides, and the active, which makes it possible.

34. Cited by Evelyn Underhill, *Mysticism* (New York: E. P. Dutton, 1961), 89.

ing them to inform the Beloved that it sickens (intellect), suffers (will), and dies (memory):[35]

> the discreet lover does not care to ask for what she lacks and desires, but only indicates the need, that the Beloved may do what He please.

The insistent petitions are heard by the "wounded stag" who grants the soul a glimpse of Himself in the waters of faith on which He is mirrored. This is the reverse of the Plotinian Narcissus image. Instead of falling into matter, where it is reflected, the soul turns, not to its own reflection, but to the reflection of God, mirrored on the waters of faith.

Love breeds itself, replenishes itself.[36] It is a continuous exercise in autogenesis that goes beyond the traditional division of love into *philia, eros,* and *agape.*[37] Strictly speaking, God loves us so that we can love Him by means of His own love.[38] The soul, placed above the "flood waters" — the suffering caused by God's absence — is provided with habitual peace and encouraged to continue its journey to God which, in the terms of Aristotelian physics, St. John calls the soul's inmost center.

At the end of the journey the soul is given the "sovereign favor" of *union* that places the contemplative in the intimacy of God's love; a transformation through love takes place.[39] It is a mutual surrender, a giving of love and friendship, with the soul now resting in the "interior bodega," the inner cellar, of His love:[40]

> the soul no longer goes about in search of her own gain or pleasure, nor occupies herself with things and matters foreign to God,

---

35. *Cántico,* II.8; *Llama,* 2.18.

36. *Cántico,* XIII.12.

37. *Philia* is the love of friendship depicted in Plato's *Gorgias* as a type of cosmic adhesive cementing nature, humans, and gods together (*Gorgias* 508a). *Eros* is the impulse of the imperfect toward the perfect in search of fulfillment (*Symposium* 206e ff.). *Agape* is the Christian love that transcends the limits of temporality (I Corinthians 13:1).

38. *Cántico,* XXXII.6.

39. *Cántico,* XXVI.2.

40. *Cántico,* XXXIII.2.

and even with God Himself, she has no style or manner of dealing than the exercises of love, since she has now traded and changed all her first manner of dealing for love.

As, strictly speaking, God loves only Himself, for God to love the soul it is necessary for Him to elevate the human soul to a Divine level. He must, in a sense, make the soul His equal. The soul, then, can be said to "dress itself" in Divine Love and His intimate life — the economy of the Trinity — and, in this way, present God to God.[41] The soul's grandeur and stability has become so great that the passions have ceased to be a disturbance. The storms have been weathered, the violent experiences, spiritual and otherwise, characteristic of its weakness, stilled.

The reality here overwhelms the words. The mystic no longer touches the mundane. We are lost, and grasp for analogies and comparisons to remedy our incomprehension. As the speculative mind cannot rest content with mystery, this becomes the point of departure for often-facile comparisons between St. John and the Stoics and Nietzsche. Doubtless, there are superficial resemblances. Sanjuanist detachment is not completely distinct from Stoic *apatheia* nor is the "stripping" of the soul radically different from Nietzsche's pursuit for absolute truth which demands the stigmatization of the "all too human."

There could be a Stoic tone to St. John's thinking. The influence of Seneca on Spanish thought was substantial and to this can be added St. Teresa's pet name for him: *Senequita*. But his thought is completely foreign to Stoic cosmic egocentrism. Insofar as Nietzsche is concerned, Thibon was shockingly on target when he pointed out certain similarities between the two: both instances of "the magic of the extreme," both thirsted for absolute truth and superhuman plenitude, and both were scavengers of masks and illusions.[42] But while Nietzsche remains trapped in the voracious maw of his own ego, St. John denies his ego as one of the preliminary moves to ascend to God. The virtues, hard and

41. *Cántico*, XXXII.6.
42. Gustave Thibon, *Nietzsche ou le Déclin de L'Esprit* (Paris: Fayard, 1975), 153-54, 173.

brittle in the Stoics, pragmatically inhuman in Nietzsche, lose, for St. John, on the highest level, their weaknesses while retaining their strength and perfection.[43]

What many critics miss and admirers tend to forget is that the entire ascent to God and its impedimenta are ensconced within Christian belief and have as their point of departure "the unfathomable mystery of the dereliction of the dying Christ."[44] Edith Stein reduces the *"camino de las nadas"* to a glaring simplicity. Our good is union with God. Our way is the crucified Christ with whom we are to be united on the Cross. The only way to achieve this goal is faith buttressed by detachment.[45]

In this chapter we have presented an outline of St. John's mystical doctrine. It would seem at first glance that much has been overlooked, such as the fact his work is didactic, and that he proposes to provide doctrine and counsel for beginners and proficients so they will know how to abandon themselves to God's guidance.[46] This is a task that must be broached together with others, such as a clarification of St. John's philosophical stance — a complex but much debated issue — and a study of his important metaphors, and will be covered in later chapters.

43. *Cántico,* XX/XXI.10.

44. Edith Stein, *The Science of the Cross,* trans. Hilda Graef (Chicago: Henry Regnery, 1960), 18, 44.

45. *Idem.*

46. *Subida,* prol., 1.4.

CHAPTER FOUR

Mind and Heart

Observations

B efore entering into the dense thickets of the Sanjuanist commentaries it seems advisable to first enter into the Saint's mind and heart, which is to say, his philosophic and poetic foundations. This is an especially urgent task given the difficulty that his works present to the contemporary mind. It is difficult to construct a reasoned presentation out of the veritable scraps and tatters we have at hand. This impediment has not prevented the ever-curious scholarly mind from spinning a multiplicity of webs. Jacques Maritain, for example, discerns a deep, essential agreement between St. John and St. Thomas Aquinas following in the wake of the Seventeenth Century Discalced Carmelites.[1] Fray Crisógono, however, takes a different course, underscoring his debt to John Baconthorpe[2] — while Winklhofer seriously questions the Saint's "Thomism."[3]

One of the most informative (albeit shopworn) studies is that of Fray Marcelo.[4] His booklet indicates that the Carmelite Order was tra-

---

1. Jacques Maritain, *The Degrees of Knowledge* (New York: Scribners, 1959), 319.

2. Crisógono de Jesús Sacramentado, OCD, *San Juan de la Cruz: su obra científica y su obra literaria*, 2 vols. (Madrid: Mens. De Sta. Teresa, 1928), 2.

3. A. Winklhofer, *Die Gnadenlehre in der Mystik des Hl. Johannes vom Kreuz* (Freiburg, 1936).

4. Marcelo del Niño Jesús, OCD, *Apuntes Históricos sobre la Filosofía en la Orden Carmelitana* (Burgos: El Monte Carmelo, 1928), 16, 30-32.

ditionally independent, not Thomistic, that the major theologians differed from Aquinas on issues such as the real distinction between essence and existence, the necessity of intelligible forms, and the unity of the substantial form. This orientation characterized the Calced until the encyclical *Aeterni Patris* (1879). Although Fray Marcelo characterizes the Discalced as faithful disciples of St. Thomas, he duly acknowledges the presence of Baconthorpe in the works of St. John.[5] That the Saint's intellectual formation took place as a Calced could explain divergences from St. Thomas.

The most prudent (and possibly the most correct) evaluation has been given by Henri Sanson: "the most that can be affirmed without fear of error is that Sanjuanist thought is tributary to all the apparatus of scholastic schemas and conceptions."[6] The data at hand indicates that St. John professed an eclectic Christian Aristotelianism with minor Neoplatonic accretions. There are many points of contact with Aquinas and a few with Baconthorpe, with departures from both. His philosophic thought was scarcely the product of systematic composition, nor is it, as has been suggested, a product of the emasculated Thomism generated by the condemnation of 1277.[7] He seems to pick and choose according to the purpose at hand with his usual fine sense of discrimination. This is evidenced by his use of scholastic aphorisms. They are cited nearly twenty times while individuals are cited infrequently. Dean Inge, in spite of chilling misconceptions, was on the mark when he observed that the point of departure of Spanish mysticism "is not the notion of Being or of unity, but the human soul seeking reconciliation with God."[8]

St. John takes the *tabula rasa* theory of cognition for granted, placing himself comfortably within the confines of Christian Aristotelianism:[9]

5. *Ibid.*, 39.

6. Henri Sanson, *El Espíritu Humano según San Juan de la Cruz* (Madrid: Rialp, 1962), 21.

7. Refer to Étienne Gilson, *History of Christian Philosophy in the Middle Ages* (New York: Random House, 1955), 402ff.

8. W. R. Inge, *Christian Mysticism* (Cleveland: Meridian, 1964), 213-14.

9. *Subida*, I.3.3.

as the scholastic philosophers say, the soul is like a "tabula rasa" when God infuses it into the body, (so that) . . . it would be ignorant without the knowledge it receives through the senses.

This is a commonplace that could have been read in any number of texts, St. Thomas' included. Aquinas follows Aristotle who, speaking of passivity *(to pathein)*, states that "mind is in a sense potentially whatever is thinkable . . . what it thinks must be in it as characters may be said to be on a writing-tablet, on which, as yet, nothing has been written."[10]

The Saint compares the five external senses to windows that receive light and illuminate a room. There are no other channels by which the soul is able to come into contact with the external world. He cites the Scholastic apothegm: *"ab obiecto et potentia paritur notitia."* Knowledge arises in the soul from the cognitive power and the perceived object.[11] Another follows: *"nihil est in intellectu quod prius non fuerit in sensu,"* which abolishes any possible immanentism. He gives the example of a man blind from birth, who, when he heard the word "yellow," would be limited to grasping the name,[12] a thesis which would be questioned by Gestalt psychology.

Albeit the universal medium of access, the senses are restricted to accidents; they grasp only the rind not the essence: only the "form," "figure," and "image." Open to external activity they pass on these forms, figures, and images — districts outside of the city walls[13] to the interior senses that act as a "gathering place" for them. Among these internal senses St. John, differing from Aquinas, distinguishes the imagination from the fantasy: "they are of service to each other . . . the one is discursive, the other forms the images."[14] Thus the Phantasy elaborates the images and presents them to the Imagination, which uses them in its discursive function. This is clearly different from St. Thomas' view that

---

10. *De Anima* 429b29-430a1; *Summa Theologica* I.84.3; *In de Anima* III.IV.722.
11. *Subida,* I.3.2.
12. *Ibid.,* III.20.2; III.13.4.
13. *Cántico,* XVIII.7.
14. *Subida,* II.12.3.

identifies imagination and fantasy: *"phantasia sive imaginatio,"* which serves *"quasi Thesaurus quidam formarum per sensum acceptarum."*[15]

True, this distinction is not made explicit in several texts — which in turn led Bede Frost to deny it.[16] It is omitted in these texts merely for the sake of convenience: "this should be remembered if we do not mention them explicitly."[17] This resembles a theory attributed by St. Thomas to Avicenna[18] who cut a swath in the "Carmelite School" of the fourteenth and fifteenth centuries.

Phantasy and imagination have another function that is exercised in unison with the memory. It is the "archive" or "receptacle" where intelligible forms and images are lodged.[19] It presents them to the intellect that makes a judgment concerning them. On the contrary, St. Thomas insists that the content of this *quasi Thesaurus* is restricted to sensible forms.[20] The intelligible forms reside in the intellective part of the soul.[21] There are then two containers of forms, the imagination and the memory, while for St. John the phantasy-imagination-memory complex is the archive of both sensible and intelligible forms.

Here St. Thomas offers a valuable suggestion. If the essence of memory resided in the past as past it would then pertain to the sensitive and not in the intellective soul.[22] This dovetails with St. John's insistence that memory is an autonomous faculty distinct from the intellect[23] and is supported by his comparison of the phantasy-imagination-memory complex to the surface of a mirror in which "the forms are seen as one looks at it" though "in the course of time they become more remote."[24]

---

15. *Summa Theologica* I.78.4; *De Anima* 429a1-2.

16. Bede Frost, *St. John of the Cross* (London: Hodder & Stoughton, 1937), 127.

17. *Subida,* II.12.3.

18. *Summa Theologica* I.78.4.

19. *Subida,* II.16.2; *Llama,* III.69.

20. *Summa Theologica* I.78.4.

21. *Summa Theologica* I.79.6; I.79.6 *ad* 1: I.79.7.

22. *Summa Theologica* I.79.6.

23. *Subida,* II.1.1; *Llama,* 50 *et al.*

24. *Subida,* II.24.5.

The intellect possesses two parts or aspects, the active and the passive. The Active Intellect "works on the forms, phantasies and apprehensions of the corporeal faculties" producing the (natural) knowledge that resides in the Passive Intellect. The knowledge acquired through mystical contemplation is far different. It is received in the Possible or Passive Intellect "which . . . receives passively only substantial knowledge."[25] Infused by God, it completely bypasses the Active Intellect.

Although the Saint does not put natural knowledge in doubt he does circumscribe it within narrow limits, as he believes that it presents a special danger to the contemplative. He seems to view it as possibly leading to an exacerbated form of *curiositas,* intellectual concupiscence:[26]

> the spiritual person allowing himself this knowledge . . . will necessarily be the victim of many falsehoods. Often the true will appear false and the certain doubtful . . . since we scarcely know one truth radically.

This is a devastating indictment. Hardly knowing one truth radically condemns us to float on the surface of reality. This goes further than St. Thomas' similar view that the nature of things cannot be known by the human mind: *"principia essentiali rerum sunt nobis ignota."*[27]

The appetites and desires that darken the powers of the soul are compared by the Saint to "murky air and water," to "nymphs" endeavoring to merge the superior part of the soul with the inferior, sensuous part. Moral and spiritual purification is able to muzzle these nymphs, arrive at detachment and at a clear knowledge of things. Strange to say, an apposite example is Satan. As it is passionless, it can easily deduce a particular effect from a specific cause.[28] While Aquinas attributes knowl-

25. *Cántico,* XXXIX.12.
26. *Subida,* III.3.2.
27. *In de Anima* I.1.15; *Quaestio disputata de spiritualibus creatures,* II, *ad* 3.
28. *Subida,* II.21.7-8.

edge by composition and division to human beings and knowledge by essences to angels (and hence devils)[29] St. John maintains that all rational beings have the same type of knowledge: by causes.

No matter how satisfactory knowledge through causes may be, whoever derives satisfaction from it, the Saint maintains, is no better than a dog hungrily devouring crumbs from God's table.[30] Because of the poverty and paucity of natural knowledge and because God transcends knowledge by causes, the Saint follows the path previously taken by the Pseudo-Denis:[31]

> We must not then dare to speak, or indeed, to form any conception of the hidden superessential Godhead, except those things that are revealed to us from Holy Scripture.

Sacred Scripture provides the tool necessary to surpass reason and move in the direction of union with God. St. John possessed an exceptional knowledge of the Bible, having assimilated it through meditation, liturgy, and the observances of the Carmelite Rule. It was not, as Bouyer has maintained, the result of a resuscitated humanistic tradition captained by Erasmus and his followers.[32] Vilnet, following in the steps of Marcel Bataillon, has shown that one of the salient marks of the *Siglo de Oro* was the burgeoning of Biblical culture, which was favored by the dissemination of Scripture in the vernacular.[33]

Although the Index of 1551 prohibited these translations, quotations from the Bible in works of spiritual content were allowed. Writers made extensive use of this permission. The works of Fray Luis de Granada and Fray Luis de León, for example, provided a veritable anthology of Scriptural texts. Insofar as the different religious Orders are

29. *Summa Theologica* I.58.5; I.64.1; I.64.3.

30. *Subida*, I.6.3.

31. *De diviniis nominibus* I.1.

32. Louis Bouyer, *The Christian Mystery*, trans. Illtyd Trethowan (Edinburgh: T&T Clark, 1990), 254.

33. Jean Vilnet, *La Biblia en la Obra de San Juan de la Cruz*, versión de P. M. de Lizaso, OFM Cap. (Buenos Aires: Desclée de Brouwer, 1953), 16, 18-19.

concerned the Carmelite General, Nicholas Audet — who favored the prohibition — stipulated that Carmelite houses should have daily Scriptural readings. This disposition was in force at San Andrés de Salamanca when St. John was a student.

*   *   *

Metaphor can grasp that which discursive reason, based on cause and effect, cannot. The "abundance of the Holy Spirit" cannot be exhausted by words. We are dealing with mysteries that overflow into *"figuras, comparaciones y semejanzas."*[34] Poetry is then able to vault the barriers that obstruct discourse. Fray Luis de León was not mistaken when he stated that poetry can act as a divine inspiration "to elevate the soul of men heavenward."[35] Taken literally, this role of verse is as old as mantic poetry. Boccaccio, in his commentary to the *Divine Comedy*, laconically states: "poetry is theology."[36] Dante himself, writing to Can Grande della Scala, remarks that there are many things for which we lack adequate words and are forced to recur to the metaphor as did Plato.[37] Thomas Aquinas, in his *Expositio in Psalmos*, states that when words are lacking then song is used: "the leap of the mind in the eternal breaking out into sound."[38]

Poetry can then touch mystery in its plenitude and stammer what is not transparent to reason. Inspired poetry, such as that of St. John of the Cross, is not a mere contrafactum, substituting a sacred for a profane meaning, though this was a genre that proliferated in the sixteenth and the first quarter of the seventeenth centuries.[39] Inspired poetry is

---

34. *Cántico*, prol. 1.

35. Cited by E. Allison Peers, *Studies in the Spanish Mystics* (London: The Sheldon Press, 1927-1930), 1:304.

36. Cited by Jacques Maritain, *The Frontiers of Poetry* (New York: Scribners, 1962), 224 n. 179.

37. *Obras Completas* (Madrid: BAC, 1960), 1063.

38. Prol.

39. Bruce W. Wardropper, *Historia de la Poesía Lírica a lo divino en la Cristiandad Occidental* (Madrid: Revista de Occidente, 1958), 251ff.

different, a real, though fragmentary, penetration into mystery, a "knowing" that transcends discursive reason and touches the Cloud of Unknowing within which dwells the God who is the paradigm of all mysteries.

The major poems of St. John of the Cross, the *Cántico, Noche Oscura,* and *Llama,* established his reputation as a major Castilian poet, perhaps equaled or surpassed only by Fray Luis de León. We are fortunate that his poetic antecedents are less murky than the philosophical ones. He was indebted to Garcilaso and to Boscán, the first a student of Horace and Virgil, both influenced by Politian and Sannazaro. In 1543 Boscán's widow published the works of the two poets, now deceased, in one volume, an event that caused a great stir.[40] St. John read Garcilaso as a young man, probably at Medina del Campo, through Sebastián de Córdoba's *"vuelta a lo divino"* (contrafactum). Garcilaso influenced him in several ways: the meter, the verse form (the *"lira"*), and often the stanza pattern.

If Dámaso Alonso is correct, the great dissemination of Garcilaso's and Boscán's profane verse frightened moralists who, following the example of Italy, converted the effusions of profane love into religious verse.[41] In 1575, Sebastián de Córdoba published *Las Obras de Boscán y Garcilaso trasladadas en materias cristianas y religiosas.* To the romantic poets must be added the paramount importance of Scripture, especially the *Song of Songs.* The Saint's vocabulary is eclectic. He employs an abundance of terms from the popular and rustic lexicon (words like *"ejido," "majadas,"* and *"manida"*) as well as hieratic words proceeding from Scripture (such as *"ciervo," "cedros,"* and *"azucena"*). The *Cántico* is characterized by the frequency of diminutives, the scarcity of verbs and the predominance of nouns over adjectives,[42] possibly to emphasize the static over the dynamic, rest over change, silence over clatter.

St. John's poetic oeuvre has been much applauded. Marcelino

40. Gerald Brennan, *St. John of the Cross* (Cambridge: Cambridge U. Press, 1973), 105ff.

41. Dámaso Alonso, *La Poesía de San Juan de la Cruz* (Madrid: Aguilar, 1958), 37-38.

42. *Ibid.,* 136-39.

Menéndez y Pelayo, after lauding Fray Luis de León, then refers to the Saint:[43]

> there is a poetry that is more angelic, celestial, and divine, that does not seem to be of this world, and resists evaluation by literary criticism.

Dámaso Alonso affirmed that the pagan strophes of Garcilaso are spiritualized in Fray Luis and made divine in St. John of the Cross.[44] There have been less euphoric opinions. E. I. Watkin, a student of mysticism, while he praises the *Noche Oscura* as a poem that beggars comment, faults the *Cántico* for often sacrificing image to allegory and ending its impassioned melodies on a note of discordant flatness.[45] And there have been far worse criticisms by those not in sympathy with his religious posture.

*   *   *

The metaphor is a splendid clue to the poet's thought. The usually cautious Sanson notes "all this wealth of images . . . illustrates the philosophical and theological doctrine of St. John of the Cross."[46] He does employ a plethora of metaphors that, on inspection, provide at least a rudimentary outline of his doctrine. This can be ascertained by the study of a few of the most relevant: the imprisoned soul, the sculpting of a statue, the ascent, and Night.

The soul in the body is a prisoner in a dungeon, a noble Lord in a prison.[47] It is an ancient, rather shopworn metaphor, not unlike Plotinus' "burial" and "encavement."[48] They are related to his doctrine

43. *Estudios de crítica literaria* (Madrid: BAC, 1915), 55-56.

44. Alonso, *op. cit.,* 25-26.

45. E. I. Watkin, *The Philosophy of Mysticism* (New York: Harcourt, Brace & Howe, 1920), 390-91, 397.

46. Sanson, *op. cit.,* 228.

47. *Subida,* I.3.3; II.8.4; *Cántico,* XVIII.1 *et al.*

48. *Enneads* IV.8.4.

of the Fall and probably derived from Plato. The *Phaedo, Phaedrus,* and *Cratylus* utilize a variation of the metaphor with the latter marking the Orphic origin of the belief that the body *(soma)* is the tomb *(sema)* of the soul.[49] Plato indicates that the body-prison holds the soul as a shell its oyster.[50] Philosophy's role is to purify the soul and liberate it from the body, enabling it to attain the divine nature.[51]

The only Fall that St. John is interested in is the Fall of our first parents from their primal rectitude. The human soul was thrown into captivity: "the soul, through original sin, is captive in the mortal body, subject to passions and appetites."[52] The ordered harmony that prevailed *ab initio* between soul and body is destroyed and the higher functions made subject to the lower.

Both St. John and the Platonists consider the human being to be primarily a soul. His works show a marked preference for the term *"alma"* over "man," "human being," "person," and so on. Soul *(alma)* signifies the whole person, soul and body — primarily the life-giving power, secondarily that which is vivified. In his schema, the soul can be said to possess a body.[53] It has two aspects, the sensitive and the rational, which, when considered as an aperture to God is called the spirit *(espíritu)*. The present state of the soul — as imprisoned — is not as humanity should be but only a dolorous *de facto* condition, the aftereffect of a catastrophe. In open contrast to Plato, who recommends philosophy as the key to purification and liberation, the Saint proposes asceticism, prayer, and total detachment.

This process of purification he calls an "emptying," a "voiding," one that does not depend on human effort alone but includes the community, superiors, and above all else, the grace of God. The metaphor of sculpting a statue is used to describe it: "to hew" is to guide the soul to the contempt of the world; "to sculpt" is to introduce the soul to

49. *Cratylus* 400bff.
50. *Phaedrus* 250c.
51. *Phaedo* 81c-d.
52. *Subida,* I.15.1.
53. *Cántico,* VIII.3.

holy meditation, and so forth until ultimate perfection is reached, which is the work of God alone, to enter into infused contemplation.[54]

The metaphor has an illustrious ancestry as it is found in the works of Plotinus, the Pseudo-Denis and St. Gregory of Nyssa. Plotinus invites the initiate to polish the statue of his true being, as does "the creator of a statue that is to be made beautiful." The sculptor "cuts away here, smooths there . . . makes this line brighter, this other purer, until a lovely face has grown upon his work."[55] The soul, in this way, can arrive at the godlike splendor of virtue. Some centuries later, the Pseudo-Denis will counsel "dear Timothy" that, should he wish to arrive at that darkness beyond light and to attain the vision of that which is beyond understanding, to emulate sculptors who[56]

> sculpting a statue out of marble, remove all the impediments that hinder the clear perception of the latent image and . . . display the hidden statue itself in its hidden beauty.

The Sanjuanist and Plotinian metaphors differ in style and content. Bréhier points out that Plotinus employs images of operations, actions, movements, efforts — dynamic images.[57] How different from St. John's preference for the noun over the verb, the static over the dynamic. Moreover, Plotinus seems to believe that the soul can select, at any given moment, the spiritual level on which it dwells. St. John, however, maintains that the individual can, in and with God, initiate the sculpting process but only God can bring it to fruition. As Sanson indicates, God does everything in the individual but with the individual.[58] This is nicely reflected in his brief ascetical work, the *Cautelas*.[59]

The very prolixity of the "ascent" metaphor makes an arbitrary

54. *Llama*, III.57-58.

55. *Enneads* I.6.9.

56. *De mystica theologia*, 2.

57. "Images Plotiniennes, Images Bergsoniennes," in *Études de Philosophie Antique* (Paris: PUF, 1955), 296.

58. Sanson, *op. cit.*, 192-93.

59. *Cautelas*, No. 15.

selection necessary. Following in the vein of the previous considerations, the most illustrative would seem to be Plato and the Pseudo-Denis, not excluding Plotinus whose notion of "flight" terminates in "nakedness": a flight from the one to the One.[60] This ascent, however, contains an element of what Underhill calls "autocratic self-satisfaction"[61] foreign to the Saint.

Centuries prior to his disciple, Plato left two superb paradigmatic examples: the prophetess Diotima's account in the *Symposium* and the analogy of the cave in the *Republic* illustrating the education of the guardians. The soul in the *Symposium* is propelled by *eros* (the desire of poverty for plenitude) towards Absolute Beauty, ascending upwards stage by stage.[62] In the *Republic* the emphasis changes, from the erotic to the noetic. Its motive force is dialectic, its goal Absolute Good appropriated through insight, *noesis*. This is the very summit of the Platonic world of intelligibles, superior even to Being: "the Good is not a being, it is beyond Being in dignity and in power."[63] Both ascents are processes of discernment and purification but nevertheless have little affinity to the *camino de las nadas* of St. John of the Cross.

In the Christian world the Pseudo-Denis describes a Neoplatonic ascent to a God whose highest name is ONE, "beyond Mind, Life and Being."[64] The soul, in the exercise of mystical contemplation leaves behind senses and intellect, everything in this world of nothingness and in that world of being to strain towards union with Him "whom neither Being nor understanding is able to contain."[65] Vanneste, in a perceptive study, distinguishes three stages or "moments" in the Dionysian ascent: (1) *Aphairesis:* the soul detaches itself from sensation and thought; (2) *Agnosia:* the method of unknowing; (3) *Henosis:* the elevation to union with God.[66]

---

60. *Enneads* VI.9.8.
61. Underhill, *Essentials of Mysticism* (New York: Dutton, 1960), 130.
62. *Symposium* 211c-d.
63. *Republic* 566b.
64. *De divinis nominibus*, II.10.
65. *Ibid.*, I.2.
66. Jean Vanneste, *Le Mystère de Dieu* (Bruges: Desclée de Brouwer, 1959), 48.

The Dionysian ascent resembles St. John's in working through progressive negations. There are, however, differences, even when the Pseudo-Denis' Christianity is taken for granted. The Saint maintains that the soul ascends by the secret ladder of faith, God disclosing Himself within darkness: God that is not beyond Being, but simply above the composite and finite being of creatures.[67] While for St. John the process of purification is itself darkness, for the Pseudo-Denis the soul enters into darkness only after its purification.[68]

But undoubtedly, the Saint's key metaphor is that of Night. He employs it constantly and insistently, often as the polar opposite of Flame. Baruzi judged it to be *"la plus geniale création de saint Jean . . . cette intime combinasion de dialectique et de lyrisme."*[69] He even left an interpretation *"en langage leibnizien"* of the Nights. Jacques Chevalier did not hesitate in comparing the Nights to Cartesian methodic doubt as both prevent us from adopting erroneous conceptions about the Absolute.[70]

As a cosmic symbol Night can trace its ancestry to prehistory, to chaos and renovation bringing about the emergence of a new uni - verse.[71] Philo might have been the first to exploit it philosophically, drawing from the Scriptures. But it is the Pseudo-Denis who is the point of departure for the tradition that assimilates darkness and light. His Fifth Letter marks a watershed: "The Divine Darkness is the inaccessible light where God is said to dwell . . . invisible because of its transcendent clarity."[72]

St. John was fully aware of his debt to the Pseudo-Denis. Night does not terminate in darkness. It is born of light, feeds on light, and is

---

67. *Subida,* I.4.4; II.5.7; II.8.3 *et al.*

68. Sanson, *op. cit.,* 302 n. 122.

69. Jean Baruzi, "Introduction à la Recherches sur le Langage Mystique." *Recherches Philosophiques* (Paris: Bovin, 1932), 574.

70. Jean Baruzi, *Saint Jean de la Croix et le problème de l'expérience mystique* (Paris: Alcan, 1924); Jacques Chevalier, "Le realisme spirituel des mystiques espagnols," in *Stromata* 2 (1940): 315-16.

71. Refer to Mircea Eliade, *Cosmos and History* (New York: Harper, 1959), 124-27.

72. Georges Morel, *Le Sens de l'Existence selon S. Jean de la Croix* (Paris: Aubier, 1961), 3:166-68; *Épitre V à Dorothée,* trans. Jean Vanneste, *op. cit.,* 245.

ultimately reduced to light.[73] The possible influence of St. Gregory (Dom G. Lefebvre has noted surprising parallels)[74] also might have influenced St. John to view the *"lumen incircumscriptum"* as the ultimate destination of Night and the ground for the total metaphor, Night-Flame. Night is the adumbration of Flame. Flame is both the goal of Night and the index of its vitality.

On a far less complex note, St. John's *Cantar del Alma que se huelga de conocer a Dios por fe* provides a glimpse into the inspiration which linked the mystical, the speculative, and the dogmatic:[75]

(1) ¡Qué bien sé yo la fonte que mana y corre,
     aunque es de noche!

(3) Su origen no lo sé, pues no le tiene,
     mas sé que todo origen de ella viene,
     aunque es de noche.

(13) Aquesta viva fuente que deseo,
     en este pan de vida yo la veo,
     aunque es de noche.

---

73. Refer to Crisógono, OCD, *op. cit.*, 2, 169; Alonso, *op. cit.*, 60-61.

74. *Priere pure et pureté de Coeur. Textes de S. Gregoire et S. Jean de la Croix* (Paris, 1953).

75. (1) How well I know the fountain's rushing flow
         Although by night
    (3) Its origin (since it has none) no one knows
         But that all origin from it arose
         Although by night
    (13) This living fount which is to me so dear
         Within the bread of life I see it clear
         Though it be night   (Roy Campbell translation)

CHAPTER FIVE

Nocturnal Ascent

Subida & Noche

"His life seems as it were the compensation for the glory of the Renascence Popes."

CHARLES WILLIAMS[1]

The *Subida* and *Noche* commentaries of the poem *Noche Oscura* may be considered prose analogs to the penitential life of St. John of the Cross, a life radically alien to the Western mind since perhaps the dawning of the modern era. Even his contemporaries found him to be exaggeratedly ascetic. When he was a youth his austerities raised eyebrows in a society accustomed to extreme fasts, self-flagellation, and other types of physical maceration seldom found today except in the outlands of sexuality. St. John's life and doctrine stand in sharp contrast to both the excesses of the Renaissance and the banal conformity of the present day.

Jacques Maritain maintained that St. John of the Cross meets a special need of the age: the healing of ruined nature.[2] Though in itself

---

1. Charles Williams, *The Descent of the Dove* (London: Faber & Faber, 1963), 179.
2. Cited by Bruno de Jesus-Marie, OCD, ed., *Three Mystics* (London: Sheed & Ward, 1952), 96-98.

a worthy task, a more modest objective, more in tune with the spirit of our age, is required. What this noisy, busy, ego-infatuated world most needs is silence, interiority, self-discipline, and spirituality. And it is here that the Saint can be a splendid teacher.

The poem *Noche Oscura* was probably written when St. John was confessor to the nuns of Beas between 1578 and 1581. It is a short poem, eight stanzas, each with five verses, an allegory in which the Beloved is approached by the Lover in the Dark Night, succeeds in attaining union, and describes its effects. The commentaries were probably written between 1579 and 1585, begun in El Calvario and finished in Granada. As the Kavanaugh-Rodriguez translation has indicated, the entire work of *Subida-Noche* consists of four parts: the sketch of the Mount, the poem, the first part of the commentary *(Subida),* and the second part *(Noche).*[3] The three books of the *Subida* cover the first ten verses which deal with the active purification of the soul. The *Noche* covers the same territory on a deeper level dealing with the passive purification of the soul. Poem and commentary describe the way to ascend to the summit of the spiritual Mount, the "high state of perfection" which is the union of the soul with God. He proposes to provide "the explanation of the Night to souls who pass through it and yet know nothing about it."[4]

*   *   *

This ascent is highly unusual. Though St. John will employ both knowledge and experience to explain it, it transcends human knowledge. His bedrock is Scripture as interpreted by the Church, endeavoring to study the workings of the human soul so as to determine whether it is undergoing purgation or is the victim of some "imperfection" such as depression. Purgation introduces the soul to the Dark Night, the necessary propaedeutic to the bliss of Divine Union:[5]

3. *The Collected Works of St. John of the Cross,* trans. K. Kavanaugh, OCD, and O. Rodriguez, OCD. Introduction by K. Kavanaugh, OCD (London: Nelson, 1964), 43-44.

4. *Noche,* II.22.2; Crisógono de Jesús Sacramentado, OCD, and Matías del Niño Jesús, OCD, *Vida y Obras Completas de San Juan de la Cruz* (Madrid: BAC, 1960), 405f., 413f.

5. *Subida,* prol. 7

we shall endeavor to say something, so that each soul who reads this may be able to see something of the path that he ought to follow, if he aspires to attain to the summit of the mount.

This path is burdened with difficulties — especially so as humanity, because of the Fall, tilts towards its own self-centered goals. Captive to the body and subject to its passions, the first step to be taken is to make the appetites "sleep" by means of mortification.

*   *   *

The first book of the *Subida* deals with the Active Night of Sense, the point of departure for the soul's trek to God. Night, as we have said, is a favorite metaphor of the Saint. It can signify the denial of the appetites. It can signify faith, or even God Himself, who is "dark night" to the soul. The ascent can be considered a single journey that begins at twilight, continues through midnight, reaches dawn and ends at noonday, the Great Noonday. St. John gives a pertinent analogy: Jacob's ascent of Mount Bethel to build an altar. He ordered his followers to do three things: cast away all alien gods, purify themselves, and change their garments. The point: Perfection cannot be attained solely by the practice of the virtues but requires the voiding, purifying, and stripping of the soul.[6]

Affection to creatures (darkness) and God (light) are contraries. There is a "rule of philosophy" accepted by St. John that two contraries cannot co-exist in the same subject. Because of this, the soul that places its affection on creatures becomes "less than nothing" and its progress aborted before its journey has even begun. To ascend the Mount of Perfection everything must be left behind: "God wills that there should be only one desire where He is . . . to keep the law of God perfectly and to bear the Cross of Christ."[7] Put in another way, the "Uncreated Satiety" cannot enter the soul unless the "created hunger" is expelled. In one of

6. *Ibid.*, I.5.7.
7. *Ibid.*, I.5.8.

those startling turns at which he is adept, St. John declares that God, in cleansing and purging a soul, does more than in creating the soul *ex nihilo* because disordered appetites are more resistant to God than bare Nothing.[8]

The soul, subject to the appetites, is like Samson under the thrall of Delilah. The will becomes sluggish, the memory disordered, the understanding imprisoned. Loathsome vices are incubated.[9] The only remedy is to extinguish the appetites, those voluntary appetites, which alone can deprive the soul of God. The Saint observes that a bird, whether bound by a cord or a thin string, is unable to fly. The Night of Mortification is necessary for the soul to progress. The natural appetites must also be put to rest. The Saint gives several counsels to this end, all grounded on the first: "have a habitual desire to imitate Christ in all your deeds by bringing your life into conformity with His."[10] Only when it achieves "nakedness" will the soul arrive at the center of its humility, experience quiet and rest, and move on to that state in which the human will becomes so transformed that it wills nothing contrary to the will of God.[11]

The Active Night of the Spirit presents greater difficulties than the Night of Sense as it deals with the spiritual part of the soul and enters into the "inner darkness" grounded on *"la pura fe"* — pure faith. Faith, as indicated, is not knowledge *per se,* but rather the consent given to that that is heard. Although a cloud to the soul, faith is the "secret ladder" by which the soul ascends to God and the proximate and proportionate means whereby the soul is united to God.[12]

Within the darkness of faith human activity diminishes. God takes the initiative and provides the soul with a "ray of divine light" that blinds its natural light. In a novel twist on the Isaiah (7:9) text, *"si non credideritis, non intelligetis,"* so exploited by Augustine, Anselm, and others, St. John provides a different interpretation: faith is acquired by *deny-*

8. *Ibid.,* VI.4.
9. *Ibid.,* VIII.1; IX.4-10.1.3, *et al.*
10. *Ibid.,* XIII.1.
11. *Ibid.,* XI.1-2.
12. *Ibid.,* II.3.3; V; XI.1.

ing the understanding, a negation that has its pictorial representation in the cloud separating the Israelites from the Egyptians.

St. John insists repeatedly on the incommensurability of God and creatures. The highest experience of God in this life is infinitely remote from Him. Moreover, in this life there can be no permanent union but, at best, a transitory one.[13] At this stage the soul bifurcates, with the sensitive part facing creatures and the spiritual facing God. The necessary process of cleansing and voiding removes whatever does not conform to the Divine Will. The faculties are cleansed through the medium of the theological virtues: the understanding is purged by "the cloud of faith," the memory by "the void of hope," and the will by the "nakedness of charity." He cites the miracle of the loaves and fishes (Luke 9:10-17), the vision of the Seraphim (Isaiah 6:2), and the key text of Matthew 7:14: *"Quam angusta porta, et arcta via est, quae ducit ad vitam et pauci sunt, qi inveniunt eam."*

To enter through the "strait gate" of Christ the will must be stripped of temporal attachments. To take the "narrow path" it must be stripped of everything subsumed under natural and spiritual. At the end of this path the soul will be transformed into God by love and will resemble God more than itself.[14] St. John advises that we should note carefully the emphasis in the Scriptural text of the word *quam*. It is as if Christ had said: "in truth, the way is very strait, more so than you think."[15]

A leitmotiv of the Saint is love, the love of God. He counsels that to search for oneself in God is only to seek favors. However, to search for God in oneself is to incline, for God's sake, to that which is most distasteful. This is truly love of God as it imitates Jesus' crucifixion and self-annihilation.[16] Writing to a young woman who wished to become a Carmelite nun he states:[17]

---

13. *Ibid.*, II.4.4; V.2; XII.2.

14. *Ibid.*, II.5.3; VII.

15. *Ibid.*, II.7.2-3.

16. *Ibid.*, II.7.5; VIII.

17. *The Complete Works of St. John of the Cross*, trans. and ed. E. Allison Peers (London: Burns, Oates & Washbourne, Ltd., 1953) 3:54, letter 10.

With regard to the Passion of Our Lord, strive to chasten your body with discretion, abhor and mortify yourself, and desire not to do your own will and pleasure in anything as this was the cause of His death and passion.

That contemplation by which the soul attains the highest knowledge *(noticia)* of God is identified with "Mystical Theology," the secret wisdom of God, Pseudo-Denis' ray of darkness.[18] He urges that the soul must unite with the darkness, citing Psalm 18:11-12:

He made darkness His hiding place. And dense vapor His canopy. Thick clouds come out of the Radiance before Him.

As faith is the medium of access to God, it follows that the greater the faith, the greater the union with Him.

The individual is able to obtain knowledge both naturally and supernaturally. The supernatural can be distinct and particular as in visions, revelations, and locutions. Or it can simply be confused, obscure, and general. These have their origin in contemplation birthed by faith. If called on to advance, the soul must leave meditation, which is distinct, and move to contemplation, which is obscure and general. St. John gives three signs, possibly taken from Tauler (+1361), to ascertain when the soul should pass from meditation to contemplation: inability to discourse imaginatively; lack of desire to fix the imagination on any particular thing; great desire for solitude to attend to God amorously without acts of memory, understanding, and will. When these signs are found together the soul should "enter into the path of the spirit which is contemplation."[19]

It should be noted that the first sign was denounced as heretical possibly because it seems to downgrade or even dismiss the imaginative methods of meditation that were current, especially the *Spiritual Exercises* of St. Ignatius (+1556), then being promoted by the Society of Jesus

18. *Subida*, II.8.6.
19. *Ibid.*, II.13.2-5.

that he, Ignatius, had founded. St. John had the misfortune of living in an era in which the *alumbrados* (Illuminati) of all stripes were proliferating and the vigilance of the Inquisition was being intensified. Moreover, several of his teachings, if taken out of context, had a resemblance to the more intellectualistic versions of spirituality later condemned as quietist, though Miguel de Molinos (1627-1696) was still in the future.

Contemplation, then, purifies the soul by voiding it of all forms and images. This is necessary as God does not communicate Himself by means of images, figures, or forms, but mouth-to-mouth, the "pure essence" of God and the "naked essence" of the human soul. The Saint affirms in daring language that when impediments and veils are removed, the soul, in pure nakedness and poverty of spirit, will be transformed into pure and simple Wisdom — into the very Son of God.[20]

*   *   *

The twenty-third chapter of the second book of the *Subida* is perhaps the most difficult for contemporary readers to come to terms with. It is bizarre and alien, having the negligible charm of a dense chapter from Krafft-Ebing's *Psychopathia Sexualis*. It deals with visions, revelations, locutions, spiritual sentiments, and other esoterica. One can rightly conclude that sixteenth-century Spain was exceptional in both spirituality and psychopathology. A few malicious observers have attempted to equate the two. What is startling is that St. John, after a lengthy discussion of such phenomena, both legitimate and fraudulent, concludes that they should be ignored. Even if they come from God they should not be searched after but only humbly accepted as "God will work how and when He desires."[21]

While the "letter and rind" of these manifestations should be cast aside, the love they generate should be retained. In this way, the ascent to God by means of unknowing is not impeded. The Saint gives the example of St. Peter who, though certain of the vision of glory he wit-

20. *Ibid.,* II.15.4.
21. *Ibid.,* III.13.6.

nessed at the Transfiguration, still directed his hearers to the sayings and words of the prophets.[22] This is of a piece with his distaste with miracle-mongers and neurotics fixated on particular images, prayers and devotions. He insists that God is the more glorified the more He is served without signs and wonders. Unlike most people, even most clerics, of his day, St. John never desired to witness the feats of popular miracle workers. He even helped to deflate the pretensions of several. In an undated letter from Segovia to Fray Juan de Santa Ana he advises:[23]

> If at any time, my brother, any man would persuade you, be he in authority or not, to accept any doctrine of the Way that is broad and of the greatest ease, believe him not, neither embrace it, even though it be confirmed with miracles, but seek penance and detachment from all things, and never, if you would attain to the possession of Christ, do you seek Him without the Cross.

It is not lawful for humanity to pass beyond the limits that God has ordained for its governance. Rational and natural limits exist. Humanity is elevated according to its nature from what is lowest and most external to that which is highest and most interior. Whatever impedes this ascent should be jettisoned. Moreover, concerning revelations, St. John indicates that God ordinarily does not reveal anything that can be accomplished by human effort "though He may converse with the soul for a lengthy period . . . very lovingly."[24]

Particular attention is given to the effects of the Active Night on the memory and the will. It affects the memory by emptying the phantasy of forms, images, and sensory knowledge. This effects a transition from the natural to the supernatural, a transition that, at least at first, causes certain difficulties. The Saint mentions periods of amnesia and symptoms that resemble the onset of Alzheimer's disease.[25] This

---

22. *Ibid.*, II.16.15.
23. *Complete Works*, 3:271-72, letter 23.
24. *Subida*, II.22.13.
25. *Ibid.*, III2.5-6.

results from the deprivation of images and forms, the stuff of which memory is made. These difficulties are transitory, though it is possible for them to perdure for a lengthy period. In any case, hope is generated to the extent that the memory is dispossessed of clear and distinct ideas — and the greater the hope, the greater the union with God.

It bears notice that the Cartesian criterion of reality, clear and distinct ideas, is here reversed. The world of the mathematization of nature is revealed to be the ephemeral mask of a Supreme Reality that creates and grounds it. The paradox is stunning. The more real the everyday world of individual things appears to be, the less real it actually is. Its core is not extension, a mere abstraction or consciousness, no more than spirit unredeemed.

Charity purges the will of its disorderly appetites such as concupiscence, which the Saint nicely describes as "swimming in the joy of Creatures." It darkens the soul and produces a blunting of the mind, *"embotamiento de la mente."*[26] In this he can be harsh, at least to our semipagan ears — as when he teaches that natural goods such as comeliness, bodily endowments, good understanding, discretion and so forth are no more than dirt and their graces the smoke proceeding from it.[27] However, there is a reward at the end of the purgation. The rejection of natural goods will effect a metamorphosis leading both to the greater enjoyment of creatures and a clear knowledge of them: "tasting them according to their truth, not according to their falsehood."[28]

Moral goods are loved by God and bring peace and the ordered use of reason. They can be enjoyed insofar as they are practiced for the love of God. Spiritual goods are of the highest importance. St. John states that his intention "in this work is to lead the soul by means of spiritual goods to desire union . . . with God."[29] Nevertheless, both moral and spiritual goods can engender vanity, perhaps even a lust for the extraordinary that will lead to the vice of spiritual gluttony. Even

26. *Ibid.*, III.19.3.
27. *Ibid.*, III.21.1-2.
28. *Ibid.*, III.20.2.
29. *Ibid.*, III.33.1-2.

the true spirit, which requires the annihilation of affect in all particular things, can become a casualty.

St. John counsels that a devout person needs few images or pictures as he or she should center on the invisible and search for the "live image" within — that is, Christ crucified. However, he can scarcely be called an iconoclast, as he approved of the legitimate use of images, pictures, rosaries, and other pious artifacts. He attacks "those pestiferous men" who would attempt to eliminate reverence toward those objects that the Church employs to stimulate devotion. The beginner, for one, requires sensible prods. It is expedient that they experience "sensible sweetness" and pleasure in these artifacts. This because these souls have not as yet disengaged themselves from the desire for worldly things.[30]

*   *   *

The *Noche* commentary now returns to the first three stanzas of the poem, interpreted on the deeper level of the Passive Night. The work is less didactic than the *Subida*, less burdened with minutiae and discussion of esoteric phenomena. Reading is easier but meaning lags behind: words fall way behind the reality signified. Nevertheless, at this stage the soul reaches the state of the "advanced," i.e., of the authentic contemplative, moving towards the perfection of Divine Union.[31]

This Night causes two types of darkness or purgation, which correspond to the two parts of the human being: the sensitive and the spiritual. The pleasure of the beginnings is reversed. The first is terrible to sense; the second horrible to the spirit.[32] The human soul moves from meditation to contemplation, from the life of sense to that of spirit. And contemplation is, in St. John's acute description as "nothing else but the secret, peaceful and amorous infusion of God which inflames the soul in the spirit of love."[33]

This inflammation is not felt at first, but progressively increases to

30. *Ibid.*, III.30.1-2; III.44.4.
31. *Noche*, prol.
32. *Ibid.*, XII.8.1-2.
33. *Ibid.*, I.10.6.

the point that the longing for God become so intense that the person believes that his bones are drying up, perhaps an allusion to Ezekiel's valley of dry bones that spring back to vibrant life. The dark and dry purgation of the appetite produces both virtues and imperfections. It is a Night that calls upon God to enlighten the soul with regard to its own misery and God's supreme excellence. The love of neighbor arises from this self-knowledge as the soul is aware of one thing only: its own wretchedness.[34]

With sensuality muted and the soul liberated from its three enemies, the soul enters the Path of the Spirit, the *via illuminativa* of infused contemplation. God begins to shepherd the soul. In the interim period between leaving the Night of Sense and entering the Night of Spirit, which can be lengthy, certain esoteric phenomena usually take place. This because certain imperfections still persist, and the soul is in danger now of losing that "holy fear" which is "the key and custodian of all the virtues," and lapsing into superstitious practices.[35] The esoterica of mysticism, often identified with mysticism itself, are the result of the imperfection, not the perfection, of the spiritual life.

It is by means of the Night of Spirit that the soul unites with God. A transition from the human to the Divine takes place, encompassing understanding, memory, and will. The affects are renewed in delight. Sweetness and inner pleasure is greater than before, even overflowing into the senses.[36] Supernatural phenomena are experienced but grow less as the soul advances in perfection. Through infused contemplation God teaches the soul in secret, instructing it in the perfection of love. Nevertheless, this Night is also "pain" and "torment" due to the contrast between our low estate and the high estate of Almighty God. When the soul suffers the direct assault of the Divine Light, its pain, resulting from its impurity, is immense.[37]

Contemplation overwhelms the human soul. Often, the contemplative nearly faints, believing he is being crushed beneath an immense

---

34. *Ibid.*, I.12.8.
35. *Ibid.*, II.2.1-5.
36. *Ibid.*, II.1.2.
37. *Ibid.*, II.5.5.

weight, a pain so acute that death seems to be a welcome release. The Saint alludes to Job and to Jonah in the belly of the whale, examples which illustrate that spiritual resurrection is found within the sepulcher. The soul is purified as gold within the crucible. It experiences a "great unmaking": alive, the soul seems to have fallen into Hell.

The understanding is purged of its light, the will of its affects, and the memory of its contents.[38] Although invisible to consciousness, this Night provides light; a light that in its purity cannot be seen, becoming visible only when it acts as the medium by which other things are seen.[39] St. John brings to mind the Israelites who, remembering the delicacies of Egypt, were unable to savor the manna in the desert (Exod. 16:3). The soul, if it remains under the influence of actual or habitual affect, cannot taste the delights of the spirit.

St. John compares the entire journey in a simile, probably borrowed from Hugh of St. Victor (+ 1140), to a burning log. When first set aflame the log gives off its moisture, turns the wood dark and ugly, emits an unpleasant odor. In drying out the wood, the fire expels all the ugly and dark accidents contrary to fire. Finally, the fire transforms the wood into itself and makes it as beautiful as it is itself.[40] The Dark Night both adumbrates and leads to the Noonday Sun. The road can be rocky. At the beginning, for example, the soul believes that its good has terminated, that it is full of evil "like the burning wood, which is touched by nothing than by consuming fire."[41]

Continuing its ascent, the soul practices the virtues (theological, cardinal, and moral), especially in times of great aridity. The soul begins to possess (something of) Divine Union by participating somewhat in the Divine Attributes. The soul advances from the state of burial, of blindness, to possess "spiritual eyes" that can see the "goods" of the Divine Light. The soul is cleansed by "strong lye":[42]

38. Ibid., II.6.6; II.8.2.
39. Ibid., II.8.3.
40. Ibid., II.10.1.
41. Ibid., II.10.8.
42. Ibid., II.16.7.

God takes you by the hand and guides you in darkness as a blind man, where, and how you do not know, nor can you . . . attempt to walk.

The darker the contemplation, the closer is the soul to God. The spiritual light of God exceeds our understanding to such a great extent that the soul, on approaching, is blinded while entering into ever more profound darkness.

The Saint indicates that the Dark Night is *"secreta," "escala,"* and *"disfrazada."* It is secret in that it is indescribable and guides the soul secretly to God. It is a ladder because, as the Science of Love, it elevates and humbles, rises and falls, until the soul attains quietude. St. John follows in the wake of Sts. Bernard and Thomas Aquinas in describing the ladder and its rungs, which extend into the next life when the soul reaches its acme and becomes God by participation.[43]

And in the Dark Night the soul puts on a disguise, a deceptive livery to evade the World, Flesh, and Devil. The livery has three colors: white, signifying faith to confound the Devil; green, signifying hope, to evade the world; red, signifying charity, to confute the flesh. This disguise both protects the soul and draws grace from the Beloved. It creates the proper disposition for the soul to arrive at union with God by emptying the understanding of its intelligence — the task of faith — emptying the memory of creature-possession — the task of hope — and emptying the appetite of all that is not God — the task of charity. The three faculties are changed, converted according to God, which allows the soul to unite with God through love.[44]

*   *   *

In spite of the fascination — not to say obsession — of his age with Satan and St. John's personal interest — spread over seven pages in the

43. *Ibid.,* II.19.1-2; II.20.6.
44. *Ibid.,* II.21.11.

Concordances[45] — it is proper to note that not only the Devil but also the Angels, are excluded from the substance of the soul. God dwells in the soul where neither can penetrate.[46] The soul must strive to attain that great purity that requires detachment from all created things so that it can burn in love for the Beloved "who guides the soul and makes it fly to God by way of solitude."[47] God liberates the soul from itself taking the matter into His own hands.

*   *   *

The *Subida* and *Noche* commentaries were left unfinished. At the end of the *Noche* he states that his explanation and exposition had only been half completed.[48] This raises a problem that has merited the attention of several scholars and should be addressed. Suffice it to say that the internal logic of the Saint's oeuvre and the structural nature of his thought would seem to preclude any wild variations of doctrine or unexpected leaps of speculation.

---

45. Fray Luis de San José, OCD, ed., *Concordancias de las Obras y éscritos del Doctor de la Iglesia San Juan de la Cruz* (Burgos: Monte Carmelo, 1980), 360-67, 1176.

46. *Noche*, II.23.11.

47. *Ibid.*, II.25.4.

48. *Ibid.*, II.22.7.

CHAPTER SIX

A Lustre of Heaven

Cántico

It has been noted with laudable — albeit mistaken — zeal that with regard to St. John of the Cross the poet is everything, encompassing the philosopher, the theologian, the Novice Master, the Doctor of the Church.[1] Due to the alchemy of poetry matter becomes crystalline, the sensual pure, on the summit of Eternal Beauty. This "ascensional dynamic" has also been attributed to the works of El Greco, who dematerializes things by introducing them into the very source of light. It is a gracious coincidence that while St. John was penning the *Cántico Espiritual* in the Toledo prison El Greco was nearby at work on the superb image of Christ in *El Expolio*.[2]

The title *Cántico Espiritual* is something of a latecomer. It was originally known simply as *Canciones* as they were sung and the commentary as *Declaración de las Canciones*. It was once believed that *Cántico Espiritual* was first used by Fray Jerónimo de San José in his 1630 edition. This hypothesis has since been discarded as this title is already encountered in the works of P. Quiroga. The first edition of St. John's works, published at Alcalá de Henares in 1618, did not include the *Cántico*. Edi-

---

1. Gerardo Diego, "La naturaleza y la inspiración poética en San Juan de la Cruz," *Revista de Espiritualidad* 108-109 (July-December 1968): 313-14.

2. José Camón Aznar, "El Arte en San Juan de la Cruz," *ibid.*, 344.

tions including it were published at Paris (1622), Brussels (1627), and Madrid (1630), the latter two in Spanish.[3]

The complete work was subjected to many revisions and was elaborated slowly over a period of eight years or so. The *Cántico* seems to have been the Saint's favorite work given the time and energy he expended on it. The first thirty stanzas were written in the Toledo prison, a few were penned at Baeza and the last five at Granada arising from contemplation on the beauty of God. The commentary was begun at El Calvario and terminated at Granada. This commentary is not an expansion, a continuation, of the poem. As Fray Federico Ruiz indicates, it is an abbreviation, an impoverishment of the poem, a descent into discursive reason. In St. John's words, the difference between poem and commentary is that between the living and the painted.[4]

The desolation and suffering of his Toledo imprisonment was the point of departure for the writing of the *Cántico*. Its inspiration comes from the biblical Song of Songs, which St. John succeeded in assimilating and translating into doctrinal categories. Most of its gorgeous trappings come from its eroticism, which was aided by the enchanting vistas the saint viewed during his life in places such as the Granada Carmel. The Saint was able to appropriate the strange, intoxicating beauty of the Song of Songs, transmuting the sensual into the spiritual.

Following the Biblical romance he writes a dialogue between the soul and God, the Bride and Bridegroom against a background made brilliant with kaleidoscopic color. The Bride speaks five times at length, the Bridegroom three times briefly, creatures once. The initial stanzas mesmerize, producing a high intensity that lasts for about two-thirds of the poem. It then lapses into a calm, almost like the eye of the storm, ending in an impressive crescendo.

The *Cántico* remains a source of bafflement. How can words en-

3. Gerald Brennan, *St. John of the Cross* (Cambridge: Cambridge U. Press, 1973), 90ff. Also Fray Eulogio de la V.C., "El 'prólogo' y la hermeneutica del *Cántico Espiritual*," *Monte Carmelo* 66 (1958): 25-26, n.

4. Crisógono, *Vida y Obras*, 731; *Complete Works*, 2:1-2; Federico Ruiz Salvador, OCD, *Introducción a San Juan de la Cruz* (Madrid: BAC, 1968), 23.

gendered by contemplative love be organized in a disciplined manner responding to a scholastic-like schema of dry categories? Its captivating exterior contains a rigorous ascetico-mystical teaching. Perhaps St. John provides the answer in a letter to M. Leonor de San Gabriel:[5]

> There is no room for the boundless gifts of God save in a heart that is empty and solitary, and they enter none but such a heart.

The gifts of poetry and knowledge proceed from the same source.

To understand the *Cántico* thoroughly it may be necessary (as Ruiz suggests) to study its diverse redactions. However, for the present study we have usually followed the second redaction (*Cántico* B) as it is the most explicit and orderly.[6]

* * *

The commentary begins with St. John declaring it was written with "a certain degree of fervor" for God. He discerns a parallel between God, whose wisdom and love fills reality, and the individual soul, which when moved by God "has to some extent this same abundance and force in its words."[7] It follows that the words of the *Cántico* should be read with the same spirit as that embodied in them. If not, these words will seem blatantly absurd.

Moreover, even if read in the proper spirit they cannot be fully expounded. There is always something that escapes interpretation. The Saint proposes to shed a "general light," a provisional interpretation, which is not binding and allows for others to be presented. Mystical wisdom does not have to be understood distinctly so as to generate love in the human soul; like faith, God is loved without understanding Him.[8] In spite of some forays into scholastic thought the very center of

---

5. Letter of July 8, 1589, from Segovia, *Complete Works*, 3:284.

6. Ruiz Salvador, *op. cit.*, 216, 222.

7. *Cántico*, prol. 1.

8. *Cántico*, prol. 2.

the work is Mystical Theology by which verities are both known and experienced through love.[9]

The *Cántico* covers the complete itinerary of the Christian spiritual life from its inception to its culmination in the state of perfection, the Spiritual Marriage. It touches upon the three traditional stages of spiritual life: the Purgative, the Illuminative, and the Unitive. The overwhelming desire of the Bride, enamored of the Word, the Son of God, the Bridegroom, to be united with him, is its point of departure. The Bride has been left abandoned and wounded although she has already abandoned all created things, even herself. The Bridegroom does not answer her entreaties but remains hidden in the "bosom" of the Father, the Divine Essence that transcends human knowledge.[10] Unaware of its full implications, the soul is also a dwelling place of the hidden Word together with the Father and the Holy Spirit.

The soul after distancing itself from things according to "affect" and "will," enters into itself in deepest recollection. The darkness which accompanies the ascent can be penetrated only by love,[11] and this comes from God, who does not ignore the plight of the soul, wounding it in love. There are "hidden touches of love," which pierce the soul like fiery arrows and leave it cauterized. Burning in this fire the soul is propelled out of itself, becomes totally renewed, and enters another mode of being.

St. John can be harsh. He tells us that only by abhorring and despising all things can this renewal be accomplished, forgetting oneself for the love of God.[12] The absence of the Bridegroom produces a wave of affliction that increases progressively, a malaise that becomes so acute on approaching the state of perfection that, on experiencing these touches, "if the Lord did not provide for them they should die."[13] Grace abounds, evoking heroic measures on the part of the soul.

Spurred on by the Beloved's absence, the soul employs her affects

9. *Cántico*, prol. 3.
10. *Cántico*, I.2-3.
11. *Cántico*, I.12-13.
12. *Cántico*, I.20.
13. *Cántico*, II.1-2.

and desires as messengers while also invoking the aid of the choirs of angels, through whose ministry prayers ascend to God. This does not ameliorate the situation as the absence is experienced in three ways. First, there is apathy in the understanding as God is not seen. Second, there is suffering in the will since He is not possessed. Finally, there is dying as to memory as it is deprived of the goods of both understanding and will. The soul is ravaged by a deathlike agony: "the lack of God is the death of the soul."[14]

The pursuit of the Beloved should be accompanied by the exercise of the virtues, the mountains of the *Cántico*. The soul must also pass through the banks — mortifications, penances and spiritual exercises — refraining from plucking the flowers, the pleasures of this life, as they are impediments to the detachment required to follow the strait path that leads to Christ. The soul will be assaulted by its three enemies: the world, the flesh, and the Devil, attacks that can result in the loss of friends and reputation, and will be subjected to ridicule, low esteem, and even depression activated by its renunciation of worldly satisfaction.[15] The Saint pithily summarizes his counsel:[16]

> [N]ot to stop to pluck the flowers, courage not to fear the wild beasts, and strength to pass by the mighty and cross the frontiers, and she must determine to go over the mountains and lakes, which are the virtues.

The dialogue moves more rapidly, accelerating to the point that it produces growing anxiety and a sense of upset.[17]

The initial moves on the path to union are the practice of self-knowledge and the consideration of creatures: the elements (woods) — peopled with creatures (thickets); the heavens (meadow of verdures), and the angels and holy souls (flowers). All are rooted in and nurtured

---

14. *Cántico*, II.6-7.
15. *Cántico*, III.6-7.
16. *Cántico* III.10.
17. Ruiz, *op. cit.*, 226.

by the Beloved, the Creator. God created all things with great facility and brevity, leaving in them a trace of Himself.

Through his Wisdom, the Word, His Only-begotten Son, He created them *ex nihilo*.[18] They were endowed with innumerable graces, which made them beautiful with a marvelous order and unfailing interdependence. As traces of His passing, creatures are able to reveal in a shadowy manner His greatness, power, wisdom and other Divine Attributes. Creatures are the lower works of God, the greater ones being the Incarnation of the Word and the mysteries of the Christian faith.[19] A double creation has taken place, the first bringing creatures into existence, the second exalting them through the Incarnation.

This glimpse does not satisfy the soul, as she desires to see the Spouse clearly: "in the place of these messengers be yourself both messenger and message." Unsatisfied desire generates continued pain. St. John, with his penchant for categorization, describes three types of pain which afflict the soul:[20] a wound, a sore, and a dying. The first comes from the knowledge garnered from creatures. The second arises from knowledge of the Incarnation and the mysteries of faith. The third and last, the "living while dying," is a theme found in popular *coplas* and exploited by both St. John and St. Teresa.

This unfortunate state of affairs changes when the soul is graced by a touch of the highest knowledge of Divinity that transforms its malaise into love.[21] The soul now resembles those blessed souls in heaven: those who know Him best clearly understand the infinitude left to understand.[22] Creatures cannot fully explain themselves. They speak like children, stammer and express imperfectly what they have to say. How much more distant is the infinite God. It is possible for the individual to reach its own center but no matter how deeply one probes it is always possible to probe more deeply into God.[23]

---

18. *Cántico*, V.1.
19. *Cántico*, V.3.
20. *Cántico*, VI.7.
21. *Cántico*, VII.2-4.
22. *Cántico*, VII.9.
23. *Cántico*, XXVI.8, 10, 12. Ruiz Salvador, *op. cit.*, 644.

St. John resembles to some extent St. Gregory of Nyssa who, developing hints in Philo and Origen, replaced the static unity of a Greek-based system by continued progress as the height of perfection. Since the infinite Good attracts infinitely, the desire to see God can never be completely satisfied. It cannot be brought to an end. This is clearly presented in Gregory's *Life of Moses* as well as other works, a view that Jean Daniélou considers to be one of St. Gregory's major original contributions.[24]

The impatient soul never ceases to seek remedies for its anguish. When it fails to do so everything thought, said, or done occasions further distress. The soul under duress is like, St. John observes, an empty vessel waiting to be filled, a hungry man craving food, a man suspended in the air without a foothold,[25] a nice image perhaps originating in the Avicennian slant of past Carmelite thinkers. The soul, obsessed by her quest for the Beloved, loses her taste for things that become wearisome. When the soul reaches the end of her tether and neither has nor endeavors to have any other satisfaction, then God is ready to comfort and satisfy her longings.

St. John cites Proverbs 2:4 to the effect that should the soul hunger after God as she does after money she would find Him, adding that the "enamored soul" seeks Him even more covetously. The soul begs God to reveal His beauty, "which is His Divine Essence," in this way to free her from the flesh so that she may have fruition of Him.[26] Fray José Ma. de la Cruz was not mistaken when he observed that "perhaps no mystic, theologian, or aesthete has treated the Beauty of God with more fervor than St. John of the Cross."[27]

Theology taught the Saint that God is present in the human soul by essence, grace, and what he called "spiritual affection." The latter

24. Gregory of Nyssa, *The Life of Moses,* trans., intro., and notes Abraham J. Malherbe and Everett Ferguson (New York: Paulist Press, 1978), Nos. 224-26; 233, 236, 238-39; Jean Daniélou, *Platonisme et Théologie Mystique* (*Theologie* 2; [Paris], 1944).

25. *Cántico,* IX.6.

26. *Cántico,* XI.2.

27. Cruz Molina, OCD, *La Belleza de Dios* (Burgos: El Monte Carmelo, 1949), 137, 220.

takes different forms and by these the soul is recreated and gladdened — a strange phenomenon, as the soul senses that it harbors a hidden being from which God communicates furtive glimpses of His Divine Beauty.[28] As no creature can serve as the proportionate means to ascend to God the effort to do so through intermediaries is doomed to failure and the soul is obliged to recur to faith, "the covering and veil of the truths of God."[29]

The lovely metaphor of the crystalline fount (cristalina fuente) was mentioned previously and is buttressed by that of the gold ring covered with silver. In both, the hidden Divine core manifests itself through the rind of faith that reveals while hiding. Faith points obscurely to the ultimate state in which "each lives in the other, and the one is the other and both are one through the transformation of love,"[30] a goal that at present is perceived only in hope. Unfortunately, the closer the soul approaches fruition the more keenly it feels its emptiness. It walks in darkness prodded by a spiritual fire that purges it, disposing the soul for union. From union in Christ the soul will advance to transformation in God.

The suffering is especially intense when the soul is experiencing certain mystical phenomena:[31]

> . . . at times the torture felt in such visits of rapture is so great that there is no torture which so wrenches asunder the bones and straitens the physical nature . . . unless God provided for the soul its life would come to an end.

Today we would think in terms of psychopathology. There is probably an admixture of the spiritual and the psychological. Ecstatic states, trances, visions, raptures, "tastes," "touches," and their somatic correlates such as cataleptic rigidity, anesthesia, and unusual alterations of consciousness glut accounts found in the literature of mysticism.

28. *Cántico*, XI.11.
29. *Cántico*, XII.2.
30. *Cántico*, XII.7.
31. *Cántico*, XIII.4.

It should be noted that the truly bizarre phenomena occur at the beginning of the mystical life when the human soul is as yet not attuned to the Divine action but tends to disappear in its higher states. In the *Cántico* St. John is brief, limiting his remarks to the state of rapture and proceeds no further with a nod to St. Teresa "who left admirably written notes regarding those things of the spirit."[32]

*   *   *

The rhythm of the *Cántico* changes when the Bridegroom *("ciervo")* appears on the hill through the lofty medium of contemplation, infusing the spirit of love: "Even as love is union of the Father and the Son, it also is the union of the soul and God."[33] The soul enters into Spiritual Betrothal with the Word, the Son of God, "an estate of peace and delight a sweetness of love . . . wherein she does nothing else but relate and sing of the wonders of the Beloved."[34]

The soul marches from glory to glory. Each watershed it reaches seems to be the final goal but its impetus pushes it forward to continue the quest. The Saint himself indicates at one point that spiritual betrothal is the most that God communicates to the soul yet it is surpassed by Spiritual Marriage which is itself eclipsed by the state described in the *Llama*. Nevertheless, spiritual betrothal marks an important advance. The soul achieves union, sees and tastes "inestimable riches" and understands "strange" kinds of knowledge . . . knowledge that transcends the natural order. It experiences the delight of an inestimable feast of love that confirms it in love.[35]

The soul's vision of creation is presented in a litany that reminds one of Oscar Wilde's listing of exotica in *Salome* but spiritualized and glorified. St. John is not viewing creatures in God in a pantheistic *mise-en-scène* but rather as they reflect the Divine Attributes, feeling in this

32. *Cántico*, XIII.6-7.
33. *Cántico*, XIII.11.
34. *Cántico*, XIV / XV.2.
35. *Cántico*, XIV / XV.4.

way that all things are God to it.[36] It may be called a vision of God's Being as Creator, far closer to Ramon Llull than to Baruch Spinoza.

St. John's catalogue of ships is no less than captivating. The Beloved is the mountains, abundant, extensive, beautiful, graceful, flowered, and fragrant: "these mountains my beloved to me." He is "solitary, wooded valleys" giving refreshment and rest in their solitude and silence. The Beloved is "strange islands," wonders and knowledge far removed from everyday experience: He and His ways, counsels, and works are very strange, new, and marvelous.[37]

He is "the sonorous rivers" and "the whisper of the amorous breezes." The first, the "Divine assault," which God makes on the human soul, resembles the surge of sounding rivers that fill the soul with peace and glory. The second receives a more delicate treatment. Two things are perceived in a breeze: its touch and its sound or whisper. In a privileged communication two things are also perceived: knowledge and the feeling of delight. It is amorous as the attributes of the Beloved are lovingly communicated. From this encounter a "whisper of knowledge" is generated in the understanding.[38]

The *Cántico* oscillates, as does the spiritual life, between delight and pain, between bliss, known through hope, and present distress, between a positive and a negative pole. The affirmative advances albeit with backward steps. The soul approaching perfection is especially vulnerable. He is like a person who, after a lengthy sleep, opens his eyes to an unexpected light. To strengthen the soul in its advance it is necessary that the vineyard be kept free of the foxes that threaten, the chorus of desires and sensuality. A principle that informs the ascent is again repeated by the Saint: "it is fitting that all the senses and faculties whether exterior or interior, be empty, idle, and at rest from their own operations and objects.[39]

The north wind that withers must give way to the south wind, which generates rain, makes flowers grow, and scatters their fragrance.

---

36. *Cántico*, XIV / XV.5.
37. *Cántico*, XIV / XV.6-8.
38. *Cántico*, XIV / XV.9, 13-15.
39. *Cántico*, XVI.11.

It awakens love and breathes through the soul infusing grace and gifts, "transforming the soul into a delectable garden."[40] However, the opposing forces have yet to surrender. The imaginings and phantasies of the lower part of the soul are still attempting to join the rational to the sensual, the "nymphs of Judaea."

To combat this stratagem the soul pleads with the Beloved to "look with Thy face upon the mountains," with His Divinity to look at the faculties of the soul:[41]

> Assail my understanding with the Divinity, giving it Divine Intelligence; and my will, communicating to it Divine love: and my memory with Divine possession of glory.

The faculties of the soul (memory, understanding, and will) have a unique role. They are important not only because of their functions but because they act as an index to the progress of the soul in its ascent to the Divine summit.

When the irascible and concupiscent roots of anger and sensuality are brought under control, the soul is enabled to approach the high state of Spiritual Marriage. To enter into this state is to acquire a high degree of beauty and purity as well as "a terrible strength" because of the close and firm knot between the soul and God in union.[42] This "delectable state" effects a total transformation that makes the soul, as far as possible in this life, God through participation.[43] St. John refers to it as the kiss of God. Both the soul and God appear to be God though neither changes its Being.[44] It can be said that the soul is clothed in God and bathed in Divinity.

This sovereign favor of Spiritual Marriage causes forgetfulness of all worldly things, and mortification of tastes and desires. At last the soul has reached the "inner cellar," the last and most intimate degree of

40. *Cántico,* XVII.4-7.
41. *Cántico,* XIX.4.
42. *Cántico,* XX / XXI.1.
43. *Cántico,* XXII.3.
44. *Cántico,* XXII.4.

love. Here the soul drinks of God according to its substance and faculties. It drinks wisdom and knowledge according to the understanding, the sweetest love according to the will, and, according to the memory delight in the recollection of glory.[45]

St. John's teaching on the Spiritual Marriage might well be the point of departure for wild comparisons with Nietzsche. The soul becomes, the Saint indicates, in a certain manner what Adam was in his innocence. He does not know what evil is, does not understand it, and does not judge anything to be evil. He is able to witness evil acts and "not be able to understand that they are so, because he has no habit of evil whereby to judge it."[46] God has uprooted the imperfect habits of the soul by means of the perfect habit of true wisdom. The person is loath to interest himself in the affairs of others, especially when it does not concern spiritual profit.

The transformation of the soul in God makes it conform to His simplicity and purity, purged of figures and forms, enlightened by simple contemplation.[47] This soul is, in a sense, beyond good and evil though it would be better to say that, being fully immersed in the Good, the soul cannot come to grips with that which has no being — that is, evil. Even in the exercise of the practical virtues it retains its strength while losing the sensibility usually linked to it.

When the soul attains Spiritual Marriage it is taught a "delectable science," mystical theology or contemplation. All its exercise is that of love, the *raison d'être* of human life. The Bride receives blessings that beautify, enrich and enlighten her as the sun makes resplendent whatever it touches with its rays. In a letter to M. María de Jesús from Segovia (July 18, 1589) the Saint writes:[48]

> The Bride sits before her Beloved, the Son of God, with the desire to be translated by Him out of the Spiritual Marriage . . . to the glorious Marriage of the Church Triumphant.

45. *Cántico*, XXVI.5.
46. *Cántico*, XXVI.14.
47. *Cántico*, XXVI.17.
48. *Cántico*, XL.7.

The drinking of the clear water of high contemplation is purchased through solitude and detachment. The understanding is elevated to Divine Intelligence, the will to the summit of love and the memory to the fullness of Divine Knowledge. The soul enters more deeply into the thicket of wisdom and knowledge that is both vast and incomprehensible. St. John waxes euphoric. This high knowledge is a priceless delight, exceeding anything that can be experienced, causing the purest and loftiest joy. On these sublime heights the reader is reminded that the entrance to these riches of God's wisdom is the strait gate of the Cross.[49]

The soul is showered with splendid gifts, the pure contemplation of the Divine Essence and its total transformation in the boundless love of the three Persons of the Most Holy Trinity. In a remarkable text the Saint declares:[50]

> For, since God grants her the favor of uniting her in the Most Holy Trinity, where she becomes deiform and God by participation, how is it incredible that she should also perform her work of understanding, knowledge and love — or rather, should have it performed in the Trinity, together with it, like the Trinity itself.

Perfect union is the very center of St. John's thought and it is the *Cántico* that provides the most detailed exposition. The *Subida* and the *Noche* conclude at its threshold and the *Llama* begins at the point in which it superabounds.[51]

After citing a beautiful text from St. John's beloved Song of Songs the soul is now prepared to go up, leaning for support on the Beloved, ready to pass through the wilderness of death to enter into His glorious place of rest.

49. *Cántico*, XXXVI.10, 12, 13.
50. *Cántico*, XXXIX.4.
51. Ruiz Salvador, *op. cit.*, 637.

CHAPTER SEVEN

The Mountain and the Plain

The title of the present chapter, though bordering on the fatuous for a work on spirituality, was chosen to depict the transition taken here from the high summit of the mystical life to St. John's sometimes-tedious writings on the ascetic life. It moves from inspired verse to counsel and exhortation, from a level on which the soul is separated from God by only a thin web to those beginnings when the soul requires guidance to commence its journey on the "path of Nothings." All of this presupposes what Edith Stein writes:[1]

> Der Ewige, der alle Wesen schief,
> der, dreimal heilig, allen Sein umfasst,
> Lasst noch ein eigenes stilles Reich.

St. John of the Cross is no less than the privileged guide to this silent kingdom.

The *Llama* was written by the Saint when he was Vicar-Provincial of the Discalced Carmelites in Andalusia, between May 1585 and April 1587, nearly five years prior to his death at Úbeda on December 14, 1591.

---

1. "The Eternal who made all creatures . . ./In addition has a silent special kingdom of his own." Edith Stein, *The Hidden Life* (Washington: ISI Publications, 1992), 135.

Fray Juan Evangelista indicates that the commentary to the *Llama* was composed in a fortnight, and without the Saint abdicating any of his obligations.[2] It was written at the request of Doña Ana de Peñalosa, a Segovian widow living in Granada and a benefactress of the Order. The present work has followed the second redaction, written during the last months of his life at La Peñuela. Fray Francisco de San Hilarion describes how the Saint would daily pray in the garden before sunrise, enter to say Mass, then return to his cell to write and pray.[3]

Although, in the original Spanish, the second redaction is somewhat lengthier than the first, the content remains the same. Those additions made were designed to amplify and clarify. Fray Andrés de la Encarnación writes at the end of the second redaction:[4]

> Our Father, St. John of the Cross . . . revised the book of the *Llama*, for there are found in it many things which are not to be seen . . . in the work as printed . . . also many additions and things set down at greater length and with greater clarity.

*   *   *

The content of the *Llama* is nicely synthesized by the phrase that prefaces the Alba de Tormes manuscript of the first redaction: *via illuminativa*, the third and highest level in the traditional division of the Christian spiritual life. In the prologue to the commentary St. John notes his hesitation in broaching the theme: "I have delayed writing until now, when it appears that the Lord has opened knowledge somewhat to me and given me some fervor."[5] This hesitancy is due to the fact that things so interior and spiritual transcend the power of language. They can be broached only if the person involved enjoys a deep spirituality.

2. Cited in E. Allison Peers, trans. and ed., *The Complete Works of St. John of the Cross* (London: Burns, Oates & Washburne, 1953), 3:4.

3. *Ibid.*, 3:5; N.L.M. Ms. 12738, fol. 17.

4. Cited by Silverio, *Obras*, 4:xxii-xxiii.

5. *Llama*, prol. 1.

It would seem that the Saint's decision to discuss the theme stems from God granting him a further deepening of understanding. Very much aware of the deficiency of language, he insists that what is said in a commentary is as distant from the reality as a picture is from a living person.[6] The *Llama* deals with a love perfected and completed in the transformative state of union. He returns to the flame and log metaphor that previously had been so nicely exploited:[7]

> When a log of wood has been set upon the fire it is transformed into fire and united with it; yet, as the fire grows hotter and the wood remains upon it for a longer time, it glows much more and becomes more completely enkindled, until it gives out sparks of fire and flame.

It is precisely this ultimate degree of enkindled love that is the leading theme of the *Llama;* that point at which the human soul becomes so transformed and inwardly perfected in the fire of love that not only is it united with the fire but it has become one living flame within it.[8]

*   *   *

In the first stanza, the soul feels itself to be wholly enkindled in love, its palate bathed in love and glory. From the depths of its inmost self there seem to be flowing rivers of glory, those fountains of living water that Jesus (who is himself quoting the prophets) proclaimed would flow from such souls (John 7:38). The soul has reached the very portals of bliss. Separated from it by only a "slender web," it urges the Holy Spirit — described as a flame — to put an end to this mortal life so as to arrive at complete and perfect glory.[9]

St. John of the Cross cannot praise this state too highly. In the soul

6. *Ibid.*
7. *Llama*, prol. 3.
8. *Ibid.*, prol. 4.
9. *Ibid.*, 1.1.

that is transformed in love, the operation of the Holy Spirit engenders acts of love so precious that one is of greater worth than everything that previously has been accomplished, however much that may be. The acts of the soul become divine. This, St. John affirms, is God's language spoken inwardly to purified souls, words of spirit and life such as those found in the Psalms, Jeremiah, and St. John's Gospel:[10]

> Only the spirit gives life; the flesh is of no avail; and the words I have been speaking to you are spirit and life.

Love is never idle. Like a flame it is continually in motion, throwing out sparks in every direction. Its task: to wound the soul so as to enkindle love and delight. Love is like a living flame within the soul. Its wounds, the Saint observes, are the games, the play, the sport of God.[11] And the more interior the play the more abundantly does God communicate Himself.

When the soul reaches God with the entire capacity of its being it also reaches its own deepest center and there understands, loves, and enjoys God with all its powers.[12] The more the degrees of love, the deeper does the soul enter God and become centered in Him. These various degrees of love, the Saint indicates, can be understood as the many mansions of the Father's house (John 14:2). When elevated to the highest degree of love, the most exalted mansion, the soul will appear to be God, to be light itself.

The Saint distinguishes between two types of union with God: that of love, and that of the enkindling of love. Referring to Isaiah 31:9, he compares them to the fire of God, which is in Zion, and the furnace of God, which is in Jerusalem. The first signifies the Church militant, the second the Church triumphant. The second, superior union flows into the soul, bestowing intelligence according to the capacity of the understanding, love according to the power of the will, and delight ac-

---

10. John 6:63 (Knox translation); *Llama*, I.3; I.4-6.
11. *Ibid.*, I.8.
12. *Ibid.*, I.12.

cording to the capacity of the memory.[13] The Divine Light expels the vicious, natural darkness of the soul, transforming it. God, all perfection, wars against the imperfect habits of the soul, transforming it into Himself.[14]

St. John maintains that the most severe purgation is reserved for those souls that the Lord desires to raise to a higher state of union. However, only a few vessels can support so rigorous a cleansing. The majority (to shift the metaphor) flees from the narrow road of life, embracing instead the broad road of self-love and death. The advanced soul, aware that it lacks the complete stature of the adoption of the sons of God, lives in hope. In a superb phrase, the Saint affirms that the soul is granted glimpses of glory and love that filter through "the crevices of the door of the soul" because of the Divine touches.[15]

Only a tenuous web now separates the soul from God, a web through which Divinity is perceived. St. John mentions three webs: the temporal, which comprises all creatures; the natural inclinations of the soul; and the sensual, in which the body and soul are united. The first two can be broken by renunciation and mortification and, in this way, unite the soul to God in this life. Only the third web, the web of life, remains. It is delicate, fine, and spiritual — and subject to assault by the flame which invests it in a sweet and delightful manner.[16]

The Saint maintains that privileged souls are gifted with truly unique deaths, expiring amid delectable encounters and sublime impulses of love. The web is broken and the rivers of love within the soul begin to flow into the boundless sea. God perfects those souls He greatly loves rapidly, taking them away before their time. The Saint's language verges on the muscular: God assaults the soul to purify and disengage it from the flesh making it divine.[17]

*   *   *

13. *Ibid.*, I.16-17.
14. *Ibid.*, I.23.
15. *Ibid.*, I.28.
16. *Ibid.*, I.29, 32.
17. *Ibid.*, I.35.

The key terms of the second stanza are "burn," "hand," and "touch," which conjoined signify the Holy Trinity: the Holy Spirit (burn), the Father (hand), and the Son (touch). They transform death into life, incorporating the soul into themselves. The Holy Spirit is the source of the "delectable wound," the Son of the "desire for eternal life," and the Father of the "transformation of the soul."[18] The Saint strains the possibilities of language in a not completely successful attempt to describe the reality of God's operations in the soul:[19]

> . . . this fire of God is so vehement and consuming that it would consume a thousand worlds more easily than fire consuming flax. It does not consume the soul . . . but rather, in proportion to the strength of love, it delights and glorifies it, a burning in it sweetly.

As this fire is infinite it fills the soul in proportion to the soul's capacity. This is the highest degree of perfection that the soul can attain in this life.

At the beginning of the spiritual life, the soul feels within itself something like a small grain the size of a mustard seed, burning and full of power, radiating this fire of love. "Seas of loving fire" permeate the soul. It seems that "the whole universe is a sea of love in which it is engulfed . . . a vast fire . . . emanating from that small point in the heart of the spirit."[20] The parable of the Kingdom is nicely transferred to the life of the individual soul.

These effusions are interspersed with warnings concerning the deleterious effects of the corruptible body on the soul. It is able to disfigure natural reason that, if relied upon, can lure the soul away from authentic spirituality. However, it is possible for the body to be affected favorably by the soul. The unction of the spirit sometimes overflows into the body, a phenomenon that is enjoyed by every part of the body down to the very bones and marrow and can be felt in the remotest extremities.[21]

18. *Ibid.*, II.1.
19. *Ibid.*, II.3.
20. *Ibid.*, II.10.
21. *Ibid.*, II.22.

The Saint here fingers an anomaly. How can God touch so delicately, as gentle as a soft breeze, when He is so terrible, so powerful? He answers that this unique hearing, seeing, and knowing is reserved for those who withdraw from the world and are perfected by the Lord. The *Verbum*, the Divine Word, is infinitely subtle and delicate. As St. John teaches, "the more delicate a thing, the broader and more capacious it can become . . . the more diffused and communicative."[22] The soul who reaches this exalted state and hears, sees, and knows should receive these favors inwardly, enjoy them, and be completely silent.

There are two kinds of spiritual life: the beatific, consisting of the vision of God; and the perfect, the possession of God through union. The first is obtained by death, the second by the mortification of the vices and desires of the fallen nature. In this way, the death of the soul is transmuted into the life of God: *absorta est mors in victoria* (I Corinthians 15:54). The soul is keeping festival, joining in the great song of joy to God, a song that is forever new. When the soul experiences this, it can, like the bride in the Song of Songs, say: "All mine, my true love, and I all his" (2:16).[23]

*   *   *

The Saint, arriving at the third of the four stanzas, seems to have reached a crossroads. His impressive gift for commentary stalls, to the point that he pleads for Divine aid, which is "very needful if I am to explain the profound meaning of this stanza."[24] The stanza is dominated by the great metaphor of lamps of fire. Lamps have two properties: to give light and to give heat, and they signify the Divine Attributes. Not unlike secular thinkers such as Spinoza, St. John credits God with an infinite number of attributes, of most of which humankind has no knowledge. Each attribute is God. Each lamp gives light and heat. From

22. (Knox translation); *Llama*, II.19, 21.
23. (Knox translation); *Llama*, II.32-36.
24. *Ibid.*, III.1.

each the soul receives knowledge and each enkindles it in love. All lamps are one Lamp and this is God.[25]

The delight generated by the fire of these lamps is "wondrous" and "boundless." The heat of one lamp adds to the flame of another. Each becomes one light and one fire.[26] This variation on the Christian conception of the Divine Attributes bears a great similarity to Ramon Llull's theory of the Divine Dignities. Llull's famous "Art" revolves around God, the "A" of creation, one with his Dignities or Attributes, which descend to created being, structured in degrees of reality and existence, corresponding to their proximity to the Dignities.[27] The point of departure for Llull's thought was the *Contemplació en Deu,* a bulky work in which speculation alternates with the elaboration of mystical techniques.

The Saint declares that the lamps of fire are also living waters hidden in the veins of the soul that quench the spirit's thirst. Again reaching the limits of language, St. John, while affirming that the transformation of the soul in God is indescribable, can say that "the soul has become God of God by participation in His attributes — those lamps of fire."[28] The lamps cast shadows. For example, the fresh beauty of nature is a shadow of the Lamp of Divine Beauty. The soul will see the wheel that appeared to the prophet Ezekiel: the Wisdom of God, a multiplicity of eyes within and without, signifying the Divine Attributes (Ezekiel 1:15-28).

A further metaphor of importance to the third stanza is that of "the deep caverns of sense," which represent the faculties of the soul: memory, understanding, and will. Through their medium the soul can enjoy a "deep perception" and experience the grandeurs of God. They are deep as they are able to receive the splendors of the Lamps of Fire and can be filled only by the infinite.[29] Humankind is decidedly *capax*

25. *Ibid.,* III.2-3.

26. *Ibid.,* III.5.

27. Refer to Erardo W. Platzeck, OFM, "La Combinatoria Luliana," *Revista de Filosofía* (Madrid), no. 13 (1953): 135f.; no. 14 (1954): 126; *Llama,* II.19, 21.

28. *Llama,* III.8.

29. *Ibid.,* III.18, 69.

infiniti. The faculties suffer when empty, delight when filled with God. To become aware of its emptiness the soul must be purged of creature affection. Then, their hunger, thirst, and yearning become unbearable.

The Saint's lyric flame flickers. The reader, who has been led to the threshold of the sublime carried along by a lyric rhythm become hypnotic to the point that feeling is in the process of outdistancing understanding, is brusquely returned to the gray on gray of the mundane. St. John launches into a lengthy discussion on the perils and aberrations of spiritual direction. Though this section is not without interesting, even illuminating, passages, it does not cover new ground, intent on applying basic principles to the field of praxis and religious counsel. He does, however, return to the notion of "shadow," urging that the human soul is a shadow of God through the transformation of union. The soul is even able to bestow a gift on God: "giving God in God to God Himself."[30]

*   *   *

St. John, in his commentary to the fourth stanza, begins by taking a look backwards to the inception of the spiritual life: the awakening of the soul. This brings the greatest blessing to the soul, as it is a movement of the Word in the substance of the soul, so great that[31]

> . . . it seems to the soul that all the balms and perfumed spices and flowers in the world are mingled . . . that all the kingdoms . . . of the world and all the powers and virtues of heaven are moved.

The soul is able to see that all creatures, both above and below, have their life, strength and duration in Him, knowing that God, in His own Being, is all things in an infinite and preeminent way. Paradoxically, things are better understood in God's Being than in themselves. This marks the great delight of the awakening: to know creatures through

30. *Ibid.*, III.78.
31. *Ibid.*, IV.4.

God and not God through creatures.[32] This is essential knowledge: to know the effects through the cause. It awakens the soul from the "sleep" of natural vision to the "wakefulness" of supernatural vision.

Once awakened, "in one single glance the soul sees that which God is in Himself and that which He is in creatures."[33] There occurs a communication of the excellence of God in the substance of the soul that strengthens the soul, making it truly powerful. The King of Heaven shows Himself as an equal, as a friend. This banishes fear. The Lord touches the human soul with the scepter of His Majesty, embracing it as a brother:[34]

> The soul beholds the royal vesture and perceives its fragrance: it observes the splendor of gold which is charity; it sees the glittering of precious stones, which is the knowledge of created substances, both higher and lower; it looks upon the face of the Word which . . . clothes her, so she may be transformed in these virtues of the King of Heaven.

In the state of perfection, that is, of union, the Beloved dwells secretly in the soul that experiences such an intimate embrace. God also dwells in other souls, but they are not conscious of His presence except when experiencing "delectable awakenings." Again the Saint stops short. Were he to speak of an experience that transcends description, it would appear to be less than what it is in reality. Commentary is left behind. St. John launches into a paean to the breathing of the Holy Spirit:[35]

> This breathing being full of blessing and glory, the Holy Spirit, wherein He has inspired it with love for Himself, which transcends all descriptions and all sense, in the deep things of God, to whom be honor and glory. Amen.

32. *Ibid.*, IV.5.
33. *Ibid.*, IV.7.
34. *Ibid.*, IV.13.
35. *Ibid.*, IV.17.

*   *   *

Aside from the *Cántico* A & B, the *Noche Obscura,* and the *Llama,* St. John wrote ten other poems of unequal length and quality (*Crisógono* #5-14), several of which are pertinent to the present theme. Most were written under extremely adverse conditions while he was a prisoner at Toledo. We have previously cited the *Cantar del Alma que se huelga de conocer a Dios por fe* with its refrain *"aunque es de noche"* (although it is night). To this must be added an eerie poem written after an ecstasy that the Saint experienced at Segovia, written in 1584: *Coplas del mismo hechas sobre un éxtasis de harta contemplación.* Several of his poems *a lo divino* hold interesting possibilities but as the Saint did not write commentaries to them it would be presumptuous to do so.

*   *   *

The distance between the *Llama* commentary and St. John's ascetic works is considerable. Nevertheless, these ascetic works provide the scaffolding for his spirituality as well as the point of departure for his mystical flights. Allison Peers observes that although these works are crumbs fallen from the Saint's table, the table is well-furnished and so completely unified that even those familiar with the great commentaries would deeply regret their loss.[36] The Saint had a liking and a talent for condensed maxim-like expressions, an important tool of his spiritual apostolate. As Novice Master and director of souls he counseled a large number of persons, a task that began with his tenure as confessor of the Discalced Carmelite nuns at Ávila.

Although probably a large number of these counsels have been lost, their number was surely extensive. Some were formal and tilted to the impersonal, such as the *Cautelas* (Cautions). This opuscule, divided into nine sections, alerts religious against the three principal enemies of the human soul: the world, the flesh, and the devil.[37] A further work,

---

36. *Complete Works,* ed. Peers, 3:217.

37. Crisógono de Jesús and Matías del Niño Jesús, *Vida y Obras Completas de San Juan de la Cruz* (Madrid: BAC, 1960), 1117 n. 1; *Complete Works,* ed. Peers, 3:218-19.

actually a lengthy letter, known as *Cuatro Avisos* (Counsels to a Religious), addressed to a Discalced Carmelite religious, parallels the *Cautelas*.[38] Another work arose from the Saint's custom of giving penitents slips of paper on which brief maxims were written. These are known as *Dichos de Luz y Amor* (Sayings of Light and Love).[39]

These works, as with all of the Saint's writings, are directed to attain perfection and arrive at union with God. The *Cautelas* was one of the first of his writings, penned when he retired to El Calvario and acted as confessor to the nuns at Beas (1578-1579). It first appeared in a Latin translation of the Saint's works published at Cologne in 1639 and later in a Spanish edition published at Barcelona (1693). The *Cuatro Avisos*, first published in the Toledo edition of 1912, was venerated at the Discalced convent of Bujalence (Córdoba) until 1936. There is a problem regarding the *Dichos de Luz y Amor*. It is difficult to determine which of these apothegms originated with St. John and which are due to the zeal of his penitents. Fray Gerardo reproduced the most authoritative collection, the Andujar manuscript, in 1913 (Toledo).

*   *   *

The *Cautelas* are meant to cultivate recollection, silence, detachment, and poverty of spirit so as to arrive at the "peaceful refreshment" of the Holy Spirit and union with God. The Saint discusses the evils besetting the human soul that are caused by its enemies (the world, the devil, and the flesh) and endeavors to provide the necessary antidotes. The world, he maintains, is the easiest to vanquish; the devil the most difficult to understand; the flesh the most tenacious and perduring. The three are linked closely together to the point that to conquer any of them it is necessary to conquer all three. If this is accomplished, conflict is expelled from the soul.[40] The *Cautelas* provides three cautions against each enemy. The following, with apologies to Professor Peers, is an edited version of his translation:

38. Crisógono, *Vida y Obras*, 1121 n. 7; *Complete Works*, ed. Peers, 3:227.
39. Crisógono, *Vida y Obras*, p. 1125 n. 1; *Complete Works*, ed. Peers, 3:234.
40. *Cautelas*, Nos. 3, 4.

113

1. *Against the World:*[41] (a) Have equal love for all persons, even relations. Do not think of them, either for good or for evil. Flee from them as far as you, in charity, can. (b) Abhor all kinds of possession and have no care for them: food, clothing . . . or any created thing. Following these cautions silence and peace are obtained and the soul is directed to higher things. (c) In the monastery guard yourself against evil. Keep yourself from thinking about what occurs in the community and assiduously keep yourself from speaking about it. Although you live among devils God desires that you abandon their affairs and strive to keep your soul pure and secure with God. Detachment and recollection will be achieved by following these cautions.

2. *Against the Devil:*[42] (a) Unless required by obligation or commended by obedience be moved to nothing, no matter how good and charitable it may appear. (b) Never consider your superior as less than God for he stands in His place. The devil meddles in these relationships. Keep from considering your superior's person or character and you will avoid the danger of exchanging obedience to the invisible God in his person for mere human attachment. (c) Always strive to humble yourself in word and deed, rejoicing in the good of others as if it were your own, desiring with all your heart that others be preferred to yourself.

3. *Against the Flesh:*[43] (a) You have come to the monastery to be fashioned and tried by everyone. The religious in the monastery are workers whose task is to model you: some through words, others through deeds, still others through thoughts. Should you fail to follow this caution you will be unable to overcome your sensual nature. (b) Never fail to perform good works if they be done in the service of Our Lord no matter how unpleasant it may be. Otherwise, you will be unable to overcome your weakness and obtain steadfastness. (c) The spiritual person should never consider what

41. *Ibid.,* Nos. 6-9.
42. *Ibid.,* Nos. 11-13.
43. *Ibid.,* Nos. 15-17.

is delectable in these works but seek what is toilsome and distasteful. This caution bridles our sensual nature.

These cautions are, on the whole, dry, burdensome but hardly draconian or inhuman. They correspond to St. John's ruthless logic and can be traced back to his seminal principles. Voluntary expiatory suffering is, after all, what truly unites humankind to Christ. Moreover, most of these cautions, if not all of them, pertain to the first steps taken by the beginner on the path that leads to Mount Carmel. It should be taken into consideration that as the spiritual life matures not only do more spectacular phenomena diminish as does pain, but also the soul arrives at a state in which the literal application of the counsels has been interiorized and therefore transcended.

St. John's life buttresses this conclusion. His charity for the sick and poor, his many interventions in the Order's affairs, his apostolic journeys, and his close and loving relation with his brother Francisco, truly a hidden saint, move in this direction. The hard, austere cautions seem to have been transfigured by the romance of the Divine. The unyielding asceticism of his external life was supported by his secret life of prayer in the flowering desert of his soul.

*   *   *

The *Cuatro Avisos* (Counsels to a Religious) is similar both in content and form to the *Cautelas*. The goal is identical. The Saint states that he is setting down points and maxims, which, though brief, contain much, and will lead those who observe them to great perfection. He advises the penitent to strive to practice four maxims: resignation, mortification, practice of the virtues, and solitude of body and spirit.

To achieve resignation, the religious should live in the monastery as if no one else lived there. He should never meddle, either by word or thought, in the doings of the community or the activities of individuals. To achieve mortification the religious should place the following truth in his heart: that he came to the monastery to be fashioned and tried in virtue like a stone that must be polished before it is set in a building. If, instead of seeking Christ, the religious seeks only himself, he will not find peace nor fail to fall into sin.[44]

The third counsel, the exercise of the virtues, stipulates that the religious should be constant in following his Rule, especially regarding obedience. All things, whether enjoyable or distasteful, should be done with the aim of serving God. He should prefer the difficult over the comfortable, the distasteful over the delectable. To put in practice the fourth counsel, solitude, the religious must be convinced that the world has ended so when he is obliged to engage in mundane affairs, he may do so with detachment, as if they were not. Effect no business that can be done by a third party, be constant in prayer, and let fall no thought that is not directed to God. Forget everything that belongs to this short and miserable life that passes away.[45]

These counsels are somewhat more severe than the *Cautelas*, possibly because they are directed to an individual not primarily to a religious community. Being cognizant of individual difficulties and quirks allows for greater precision and, when necessary, greater severity. In substance they are similar, nearly identical, and can be encountered interspersed in passages of the commentaries.

*　　*　　*

The apothegms that comprise the *Dichos de Luz y Amor* are brief and to the point. They can be viewed separately. Their order can be modified at will without doing them violence. Ascetic rather than mystical, they add little to the Saint's doctrine but, because of the arresting manner in which they are articulated, they hold our attention more than do the *Cautelas* and the *Cuatro Avisos*. Expressed usually in lively terms, these *dichos* have bolted the Sanjuanist corpus to become staples of religious literature. The following are taken from the Andujar manuscript:[46]

---

44. *Cuatro Avisos*, Nos. 2-4.
45. *Ibid.*, Nos. 5-9.
46. *Dichos de Luz y Amor, Complete Works*, ed. Peers, 3:241-47.

(#1) Now that wickedness is revealing her face more and more clearly, He (God) reveals (the treasures of His Wisdom and Spirit) in large measure.

(#2) The soul that is alone and without a master, his virtue is like a solitary burning coal. It will grow colder rather than hotter.

(#13) God desires the least degree of obedience and submission more than all the services you would very much like to accomplish.

(#24) The fly that clings to honey hinders itself from flying; and the soul that clings to spiritual sweetness hinders its own liberty and contemplation.

(#28) The soul that is hard becomes harder through love of self.

(#32) One single thought of man is of greater worth than the whole world, therefore only God is worthy of it.

(#57) At eventide they will examine you in love. Learn to love as God desires to be loved. Lay aside your own temperament.

(#60) Man does not know how to rejoice or grieve correctly, as he does not comprehend the distance which exists between Good and Evil.

Much of the above deserves a chronological account of the works in which they appeared when detached from the Sanjuanist corpus. However, the size and scope of the present work does not permit such an interesting but hardly substantive digression.

St. John of the Cross, at the very point of death, embraced the lyrical, asking that verses of the Song of Songs be read. In the *Dichos de Luz y Amor*, he interrupts the stunning catalogue of maxims after #25 with the "Prayer of the Soul enkindled with Love." This chapter ends with lines from this prayer:[47]

Mine are the heavens and mine is the earth: mine are the people, the righteous are mine and mine are the sinners; the angels are mine and the Mother of God, and all things are mine, for Christ is mine and for me. What, then, do you ask for and seek, my soul? Yours is all this, and it is all for you.

47. *Ibid.*, 3:244.

117

CHAPTER EIGHT

Pieces of the Puzzle

In the four hundred years since his death, St. John of the Cross has vaulted the boundaries of Iberia and the Catholic Church to become a universal figure of sorts. A strange fate touched with irony for a man who represented, as Edith Stein observed, the ancient eremitical spirit in its purest form.[1] Those who believe that mystics are a breed apart, a sort of club without confessionial ties, welcome him into their midst to join hands with Sankara, Paracelsus, Boehme, and other assorted worthies. Further, the Saint has provided inspiration for spiritual men and women both within and without his Discalced Carmelite Order. His thought has piqued the interest of diverse figures such as de Foucauld, T. S. Eliot, and Charles Williams as well as thinkers of repute such as Henri Bergson and Maurice Blondel, a philosopher who made a failed attempt to interest Père Teilhard de Chardin in the Saint's work.

Together with many other good and worthy things, St. John and his oeuvre have, in the past century, suffered from the ravages of trivialization, making appearances in books of pop spirituality and psychology. Volumes have appeared in which his doctrine is compared to the Bhagavad-Gita, selected Zen masters, and Carl Jung. In some books

---

1. Edith Stein, *The Hidden Life*, ed. L. Gelber and M. Linssen, OCD, trans. W. Stein (Washington: ICS Publications, 1992), 5.

he is even considered to be a forerunner of radical feminism or other contemporary movements. Since approximately the midpoint of the twentieth century studies of his thought have tilted to the banal, most hagiographic or contrived. Alas, this is only one example of the flood of the trivial that has become the order of the day, markedly within the confines of the Roman Catholic Church.

Charles Péguy, at the beginning of the twentieth century, predicted that a new world was coming into existence, "a quite different world . . . the world of those who no longer believe in anything, not even atheism."[2] In this world — today's world — St. John of the Cross is an alien and a contradiction. Instead of unbelief he preaches unyielding faith and instead of chatter, silence. Obedience, not self-will; contemplation, not the whirligig of the imagination; detachment from things, not indulgence in them. The tiny, ragged, discalced Friar who tramped through cold, bare, mountainous Castile would definitely be ill at ease in the canyons of Wall Street.

But leaving aside the vagaries and aberrations of the contemporary world, it may be of some interest to view the Saint and his work within the context of major issues which have faced Christianity and which still resonate in the Christian psyche. Obviously one is obliged to be selective, as religion and its apex in mysticism enters into nearly every area of human endeavor. Though Péguy's dictum that everything begins in mysticism and ends in politics may be exaggerated, it does point to a vast and complex field. A good argument can be made that three of those issues with reference to St. John's thought that would be pertinent and instructive are the relation between nature and grace, Christianity and atheism, mysticism and the rational proofs for the existence of God.

*   *   *

For the better part of a century a controversy racked Catholicism, concentrated then in the French Church, which still pullulates in its uncon-

---

2. Charles Péguy, *Basic Writings*, trans. Anne and Julian Green (New York: Pantheon, 1948), 103.

scious. It centered around different visions concerning that tenuous frontier where our finite world touches on the unknown supreme reality not limited by space or time. Where does nature touch grace, the finite touch the infinite? Finite humankind seems to be trapped between two infinities: God and Nothingness. The human being, as Pascal noted, is an "incomprehensible monstrosity," a monstrosity in relation to the infinite, a whole in relation to nothingness.[3] Leszek Kolakowski discussed this controversy in an interesting albeit slanted manner,[4] a writer whose sharpness is dulled by his antagonistic attitude to the hierarchical Church. So let us proceed with cautionary prudence to give a brief outline of the controversy in which the principal actors were the Jesuits and the Jansenists.

The adversaries were formidable. The Jesuits enjoyed a tradition grounded on St. Ignatius' *Spiritual Exercises* and *Constitutions,* buttressed intellectually by the refinement of scholastic thought by Suárez and Molina, among others. Although strong and vital it had lost much of its rigor when expounded by the Jesuit moral philosophers of the seventeenth century. The Jansenists were pietistic and rationalistic in the sense birthed by the sixteenth-century mathematization of nature. They were intellectually active, wrote manuals, published the *Port Royal Logic* and counted great thinkers and mathematicians such as Pascal and Arnauld in their ranks. Kolakowski sums up the difference between the adversaries in a pithy, if prejudiced, manner: "the Jesuits defended reason but were not defended by reason; the Jansenists were against reason but reason was on their side."[5]

The Jesuits, the casuists of seventeenth-century France, attempted to integrate the finite world and its values within the reality and infinity of God. Supernatural reality became an extension of temporal reality, not that different from the Lutheran *homo capax infinitum.* The finite and infinite are homogeneous and form part of a harmonic

3. *Pensées,* No. 72.

4. Leszek Kolakowski, "Reflexiones de sacro e profano," in *Vigencia y caducidad de las Tradiciones Cristianas,* trans. Ramon Bilbao (Buenos Aires: Amorrortu Editores, 1973), 9, 11, 13, 55, *et al.*

5. Kolakowski, "La trivialidad de Pascal," in *ibid.,* 60.

order. Religion is neither dangerous nor uncomfortable. It is possible for grace to be activated by insignificant motions. The religious life is no more than an intensification of everyday life, a life without any exceptional episodes. This converted the supernatural into a mere adjunct of the natural world, nicely reflected in Abbé Bremond's phrase "devout humanism," by which he characterized the Jesuits. This tilts towards a spiritual reductionism which has proved to be popular and today is reflected in the spirituality of large and influential Roman Catholic congregations as well as elsewhere.

The Jansenists, following the Augustinian maxim that God's greatness is revealed by the fact that He reveals Himself in a world opposed to him, maintained that there is no relation between grace and nature, the natural and the supernatural. There is no common measure to mediate between them. Nor do they express themselves in the same language. A human being exists in both worlds simultaneously, a precarious situation not without its unpleasant aspect. As Pascal said to his sister, Mme. de Perier, "sickness is the natural condition of the Christian."[6] All real worth should be denied to the temporal world as faced by the Infinite Being it is reduced to nothing. This is similar to the Calvinist: *homo incapax infinitum*. The *Pensées* is a testimony to the irreconcilability of the two worlds, a point later accentuated by Kierkegaard, who, as Przywara indicated, is Pascal's peculiar fulfillment.[7]

Two other options are suggested by Kolakowski in a later article in which vitriol is substantially reduced: first of all, that of the Thomists. This is a sort of *via media* — "dualism in subordination." That is, earthly life is the seat of evil but scarcely independent of eternal values. The Divine is the sacred aspect of empirical reality, the point at which the infinite impinges on the finite.

The final option is Teilhard de Chardin, a twentieth-century Jesuit priest, who, in Kolakowski's opinion, made the only attempt to review

---

6. *Ibid.*, 65.

7. Erich Przywara, SJ, "St. Augustine and the Modern World," in *A Monument to St. Augustine* (London: Sheed & Ward, 1945), 226.

the totality of Christianity from a philosophical point of view, a vision which "definitely leads to a total sacralization of created being and . . . an affirmation of the profane as the authentic place for the fulfillment of Christian values."[8] Actually, the Teilhardian grotesque is far more than this.

This issue transcends the speculative as it presents the Christian Church with what appears to be a Hobson's choice. If it defends the notion of the sacred as radically distinct from the profane, it runs the risk of lapsing into a minor sect struggling for survival in a world which each day understands it less. However, if it follows the option that the sacred is an extension of the profane, Christianity is in danger of being indistinguishable from the world. These two options, followed consistently, lead, on the one hand, to a remnant Church, progressively alienated from the world in which it lives. And on the other hand, to a worldly Church, scarcely distinguishable from the world that surrounds and engulfs it.

Where does St. John of the Cross stand? Certainly not with Teilhard de Chardin whose enthusiasm for evolution, a *meta-Christum* and the constitution of a *meta-christianisme*, goes far to justify Gilson's appraisal of him as the most Christian of the Gnostics.[9] Development is constant and homogeneous. Christ is the cutting edge of a cosmic evolution sweeping upwards towards its goal in Omega Point. For St. John, however, there is no divinization without supernaturalization, which is to say, without the death of nature.[10] To paraphrase Dr. Johnson on Scotland, for the Saint the best thing in the world is the path to get out of it. The *"camino de las nadas"* the path of negation, demands that the world and all it comprises be purged, negated, surpassed; and this in spite of, or perhaps because of, his great aesthetic sensibility.

The Saint's position would probably be found someplace between that of St. Thomas and that of the Jansenists. He would not be sympa-

8. Kolakowski, "Teilardismo y cristianismo maniqueo," in *Vigencia y caducidad,* 79, 69-78.

9. *Letters of Étienne Gilson to Henri de Lubac,* trans. Mary E. Hamilton (San Francisco: Ignatius Press, 1988), 128. Henri de Lubac provides a vigorous defense of Teilhard in *La Pensée réligieuse du Père Pierre Teilhard de Chardin* (Paris: Aubier, 1962).

10. Federico Ruiz Salvador, OCD, *op. cit.,* 154.

thetic to the view attributed to the Jesuits, which leads ineluctably to that of the anonymous Christian and blunts the radical difference between nature and grace. The Saint would certainly agree with the Jansenists that the temporal world, taken by itself, has no real value. Nevertheless, as God's creation, by manifesting His attributes it provides a stimulus for the soul to abandon it and enter into reality. Though he would agree that sickness is the natural condition of the Christian as everyone is subject to the ravages of original sin, this is no more than the very beginning of the voyage to the summit of Mount Carmel. As Father Bouyer indicated, St. John of the Cross brought ascesis into mysticism, "the mystery of Christ crucified in ourselves."[11]

The Creator who created all things with ease and brevity is separated from His creatures by an abyss. He left two dispositions for the ordering of his creation: traces of who He is and definite limitations. It is not licit for any creature to attempt to break out of these limitations or attempt to obtain favors through supernatural means. As human beings are obliged to follow natural reason and evangelical doctrine any attempt to know in a supernatural way is to tempt the Almighty.[12]

However, when, through hearing we believe what is taught, our "natural light" is blinded, darkened by the presence of faith. By the darkening of the natural self through negation and renunciation the soul is able to arrive at a supernatural transformation that it cannot achieve on the purely natural level. In this way, the operations of the soul are transformed from the natural to the divine.[13]

The Saint repeatedly states with bare simplicity that the supernatural is simply that which is above the natural order. The tranquil and silent spirit can by grace be elevated from the "cloud of natural knowledge" to the "midday light" of the supernatural knowledge of God.[14] For St. John the natural person is equivalent to St. Paul's "old man" and the supernatural one to St. Paul's "new man." In one important pas-

11. Louis Bouyer, *The Christian Mystery*, trans. Illtyd Trethowan (Edinburgh: T&T Clark, 1990), 254-55.

12. *Subida*, I.4.3; II.21.1; II.21.4; *Cántico*, V.1.

13. *Subida*, II.3.1.

14. *Subida*, II.15.4.

sage, he indicates that the light of understanding extends only to natural knowledge *"aunque tiene potencia para lo sobrenatural"* (although it possesses obediential potency when the Lord desires to put in supernatural act).[15]

Although the word "obedience" is a poor way of expressing the relation of nature to grace, it does succeed in fingering the connection between the natural desire to see God and its gratuitous elevation to the supernatural order. If, as St. Thomas maintained, the natural appetite of a being is its finality, it follows that all of nature tends to its end. St. John of the Cross is simply indicating that humankind's natural end, which is the vision of God, can be attained only by assistance that comes from outside nature. Only by surpassing the natural can the "enamored soul" be filled by God.[16]

There is a problem. While God, with the figure of His Son, left all things dressed in beauty, communicating supernatural being to them, we are told that the supernatural does not fit within the natural mode, nor have anything to do with it.[17] It seems that for the Saint the individual is *capax infiniti* contingent on the Divine initiative. Though closer to the Jansenist position both theoretically and temperamentally, he does have links with the French Jesuit position forged by the scholastic rationalism absorbed at Salamanca. But he is far closer to St. Thomas Aquinas, whose "dualism in subordination" with an added dollop of pessimism would be nearly identical to the view of St. John of the Cross.

*   *   *

The belief that we live in a post-Christian world has roots that go back at least to the Renaissance. Today, most intellectuals believe that it is no longer a question as it has been answered in the affirmative and there is no reason to dispute this judgment. Christianity no longer matters. It is simply another color on the palette of outworn religions. Zarathustra

15. *Cántico*, V.4; *Llama*, III.75.
16. *Cántico*, XI.9.
17. *Subida*, II.40.1; *Cántico*, VIII.3.

was right in affirming that the immodest, prying, overly pitiful witness of our most intimate secrets had to die. One recalls Virginia Woolf's letter to her sister Vanessa after chatting with the newly converted T. S. Eliot to the effect that there is something obscene in a living person sitting by the fire and believing in God. A few decades later, Vahanian observed that[18]

> the essentially mythological world view of Christianity has been succeeded by a thoroughgoing scientific view of reality, in terms of which God is no longer necessary nor unnecessary: he is irrelevant — he is dead.

This view, although somewhat outdated, received a favorable hearing even among Christians. Although "death of God" theology, prominent in liberal circles in the 1960s, succumbed to the galloping death accorded to fads, variations are still present especially in those types of thought that can be called humanistic.

The river of thought emerging from the Enlightenment swollen by additional rivulets served to center human interest on itself in an orgy of collective narcissism. If the seventeenth century marked the disappearance of God from the sciences, perhaps the twentieth century can be said to have marked the disappearance of God from human life. And if the human being is the supreme value, Christianity has become superfluous. Ironically, it was Christianity that birthed and energized this malevolent double, which, conscious of its power, declared its independence and attempted to impose its authority. On the practical level, this is reflected in the project of building a global society on humanistic grounds, an endeavor that, in Christian tradition, is one of the signs of the approach of Antichrist.

When Hegel made the Divine Essence an object subject to imprisonment in the concept, and made the full realization of God dependent on humankind, this consummated a process that led ineluctably to the trivialization of the Divine. Once Christianity placed the *Logos* in God

18. Gabriel Vahanian, *The Death of God* (New York: Braziller, 1966), xxxiii.

speculation began a wild career in which the *Logos* ended as the essence of humanity.[19] This turn is evidenced by several of Hegel's early writings. In the *Positivity of the Christian Religion* he fulminates against positive religion, one based on authority, while advocating a human morality grounded on freedom. Later, in *The Spirit of Christianity* he attacks the "Jewish mentality" identified with the otherworldly of which Abraham is the prototype. Hegel piles scorn on Abraham who is "a stranger to the earth" and regards the world as opposed to him. Abraham's God is accused of making the "horrible claim" that He alone is God. Peter's confession of Christ's divinity (Matthew 16:13-20) is interpreted as the recognition of God in humanity: the human *(anthropos)* is the light *(phos)* of the world.[20]

Not all of Hegel's heirs opted for atheistic humanism. Teilhard de Chardin, born on the wrong side of the Hegelian blanket, retains, even augments Hegel's religious tone while elaborating a humanistic gnosis with cosmic trappings. Resemblances do exist: a God who is perfected by His creation; a humanity who works for the constitution of the earthly *pleroma;* a world whose triumph is the triumph of God Himself.[21] The notion that everything is sacred, nothing is profane, a view rightly or wrongly attributed to this current of thought, became a strong presence in religious thought. The boundary between nature and grace, humanity and God, begins to dissolve.

The logical consequence of "everything is grace" is the affirmation that "God is dead." Feuerbach's maxim that theology is anthropology, the analog to the serpent's temptation in Eden, has been fulfilled. People are as gods. Humanity is divine. The study of humankind is the study of God. In the background is the Christian dogma of the Incarnation which, when distorted, is the ultimate source of the exaltation of autonomous humanity in frank opposition to Christianity itself.[22]

19. Xavier Zubiri, "Hegel y el problema metafisico," *Naturaleza, Historia, Dios* (Madrid: Editoria Nacional, 1963), 229.

20. Friedrich Hegel, *On Christianity*, trans. Knox and Kroner (New York: Harper, 1961), 68ff.

21. *Ibid.*, 186-87, 242.

22. Karl Löwith, *From Hegel to Nietzsche* (New York: Doubleday, 1967), 308.

The defunct death of God theology proclaimed that the spirit had transcended the revelation given by the canonical Bible to initiate a new form of faith that rejected worship, preaching, prayer, ordination, and the sacraments. Humankind, it urged, should be liberated from every alien and opposing Other so as to advance into what Blake hailed as "the Great Humanity Divine." They preached a present Jesus who perhaps was a dialectical process, not an existent being.[23] Although this banal pastiche has faded several of its caricatures are still with us. Humanism is protean.

Humankind, for St. John of the Cross, is always more than simply human: its very being is modified by its relation to the Divine. Humanism is burdened by a veiled envy of the Absolute, probing humanity for what can be found only in God. For Christianity, the human is, in a sense, a provisional being as ultimately there will be one Christ loving himself.[24] Creatures only serve to whet the appetite and cannot serve as the medium of access to union with God. The Saint repeatedly cites a rule of philosophy that means must be proportionate to their end and creatures simply do not exhibit the necessary accord and likeness to serve as a bridge to the Deity.

A *criatura* — a creature — is anything not God, anything subsumed under genus and species; "God is of another being than His creatures and infinitely distant from them."[25] Whoever desires to attain spiritual perfection is obliged to reject engrossment with creatures, in this way disposing itself for the reception of the contrary form, who is God. Attachment to creatures obstructs the entrance of the spiritual form and causes the soul to fall to the level of the creature on which it fixes its attention.

The soul, by its very nature, is inclined towards that which is like itself, a belief held by many thinkers, including Plato and Descartes: for the former, the Ideas, for the latter, the simple elements. The soul, the Saint

23. Thomas J. J. Altizer, *The Gospel of Christian Atheism* (Philadelphia: Westminster Press, 1966), 25, 27f., 58, 107f.; "America and the Future of Theology," in *Radical Theology and the Death of God* (Indianapolis: Bobbs-Merrill, 1966), 11.

24. *Epistola ad Parthos*, 70.

25. *Subida*, III.12.1-2.

indicates, either ascends to God or falls to the level of creatures. God is the *raíz y vida* (root and life) of all creatures; they have their life, duration, and strength in Him.[26] Of the double creation — the first *ex nihilo*, the second through the Incarnation — the Saint likes to stress the latter as it recreated humankind in complete beauty. Separated from its root and ground creation is a *nada*, a nothing. The worldly-wise attach themselves to this NADA, unable to deal with a God who is truly a stranger and because of this they hold the wise according to God in contempt.[27]

*   *   *

Demonstrating the existence of God is not a problem for the Christian mystic. It is simply taken for granted. St. John of the Cross wants to be overwhelmed by God, be inebriated by God, be rapt from this life by God: *"Descubre tu presencia, y máteme tu vista y hermosura."*[28] The hypothetical doubt, which usually precedes a demonstration on the part of the believer, was completely alien to him. The problem for him is not God but humanity immersed in the ugliness and obscurity of sin. A proof for God's existence would strike him as presumptuous. Yet his own attempts to touch the ineffable by means of poetic inspiration and discursive commentaries certainly awaken intimations of an unknown and distant realm. The difficulty resides in that[29]

> God is above the heavens and speaks from the depths of eternity; we on this earth are blind and understand only the ways of flesh and time.

It should be asked whether this dichotomy leaves sufficient *Lebensraum* for a rational approach to God, though perhaps not by means of the traditional proofs.

26. *Cántico*, XXXIX.11; *Llama*, IV.5.

27. *Cántico*, XXVI.13.

28. "Reveal your presence clearly and slay me with your sight and beauty." *Cántico* B, stanza 11.

29. *Subida*, II.20.5.

Rational demonstrations of God's existence arose when Christianity attained full consciousness of itself; faced either with doctrinal insurgency or with the imperative of missionary activity, it requires an appeal to the common inheritance of reason. To the *insipiens,* the unbeliever, these demonstrations may well appear to be not-so-elaborate masquerades, religious propaganda in mufti. To this are added the difficulties consequent on different theological schools and intramural conflict of religious orders. Moreover, even the most famous proofs present difficulties. St. Thomas' *quinque viae* are presented in succinct fashion in only one dense article of the *Summa Theologiae* and developed more at length in the *Summa Contra Gentiles.* To complicate matters, these "ways" are derived from different, often incongruous sources such as Avicenna and St. John Damascene.[30]

The usual justification for rational proofs of God's existence is Romans 1:20: *"Invisibilia Dei per ea quae facta sunt, intellecta, conspiciuntur."* This text is usually understood in the following manner: the existence of God can clearly be demonstrated from the consideration of the visible things of nature, i.e., those given in sense experience. However, thinkers with mystical leanings have, at least since St. Augustine, emphasized the importance of that highest visible created thing — humankind itself. St. Bernard clearly expresses this view:[31]

> Let us seek the understanding of the invisible things of God by those things that are made: but if the soul sees them to be understood in other creatures, she needs see them much more delicately in the creature made in the image of God, that is, in herself.

The human soul is a spirit and so is the Divine Word. As St. Bernard observes, spirits have a common language, "tongues of their own."

The Saint's understanding is similar to that of Augustine and Bernard, placing the emphasis in the Romans 1 text on "created" *(quae facta*

---

30. Refer to Étienne Gilson, *The Philosophy of St. Thomas Aquinas* (New York: Random House, 1956), 59f.

31. *Serm. de div.,* 9, 2.

sunt) not on "visible." Creatures reveal God "as through fissures in a rock."[32] Rational creatures, which are more noble than the sensible, reveal more than they do, an "admirable immensity," but without quite disclosing God. The human soul is both the most beautiful of creatures and God's hiding place. This is why the quest for God should be within and not without.[33] However, the important quest is that for union with God and this can only take place by means of the path of unknowing.

Nevertheless, creatures carry a seed of a superior order of being and an inchoate meaning which is inexpressible. Things carry *"un no sé qué que quedan balbuciendo,"* a stammering carrying a lofty understanding that cannot be put into words.[34] This seems to leave an opening for rational speculation though it certainly restricts its scope. In the *Cántico* St. John goes on at length concerning the longings of the soul caused by the Bridegroom's absence. As we have seen, he uses three metaphors; the first is *herida* (wound) and arises from the knowledge that the soul receives from creatures; the second, *llaga* (sore), is caused by knowledge of the Incarnation; the third, *morir* (dying), is produced by the perception of the *no sé qué* that lies behind the stammering of creatures.[35] The first could possibly be the point of departure for a demonstration of the existence of God in the traditional mode as it is basically a lyric version of Romans 1:20.

The question arises: why did St. John not attempt to formulate a proof? Perhaps because he was convinced that any comparison between creature and Creator entails the interpretation of the latter in terms of the former and this might lead to the fabrication of a straw god separated by an abyss from the living God given in Christian faith. Nevertheless, several traditional proofs, if correctly understood, escape this fate.

It is often forgotten that, in spite of extravagant interpretations of his *quinque viae* St. Thomas was primarily attempting to demonstrate

---

32. *Cántico,* VI.6.
33. *Cántico,* VII.1; I.7; *Subida,* II.5.3.
34. *Cántico,* VII.9.
35. *Cántico,* VII.2-4.

that the proposition "God exists" is true. He leaves God's essence and mode of existence in respectful obscurity.[36] St. Thomas ended his life of rational speculation with the discovery of silence — St. John of the Cross' point of departure.

*   *   *

The three issues just discussed were selected arbitrarily though not randomly. They are intended to show that St. John of the Cross has something valuable to say concerning problems which, at least in some way, are still with us, that he still serves as a source of inspiration. He reminds us that God is not dead though he may be a dark night to us in this life. St. John of the Cross allows us to discern under the deadening noise and chatter of a rebellious world, the disturbing presence of "that single bliss and sole felicity."

---

36. *Summa Theologiae* 1.3.4 *ad* 2; 1.12.12 *ad* 1.

CHAPTER NINE

Odds and Ends

M any objections have been launched against the doctrine set
forth in the works of St. John of the Cross. It has been called
harsh, uncompromising, lacking in humane values, alien to the modern world. The scene he depicts is frightening: a God so distant as to
be unknowable; a world that is menacing and corrupt; a soul that
lusts for divinity but teeters on the brink of nothingness, experiencing terror and anguish, ameliorated by a hope, which, even to the
mystic, often seems ephemeral. To this may be added what can be
considered a sadomasochistic attachment to severe penances, physical maceration, relic-veneration, and the frenzied pursuit of the
physical remains of reputedly holy men and women that verges on
the cannibalistic as the post-mortem fate of both St. Teresa and St.
John attests.

Furthermore, it can be proposed that St. John of the Cross and his
oeuvre were the products of a unique milieu permeated with the fanaticism of the Counter-Reformation. This blended with alien elements
such as Neoplatonism, which infiltrated Christianity at an early stage
and generated contempt for material creation and the human body.
These elements were stamped on the medieval consciousness and
passed into sixteenth-century Iberia. Moreover, with the Spanish rejection of the pagan aspects of the Renaissance and the return-to-origin

aspirations of the Reformation the peninsula entered modernity as an avowed enemy. Is it possible to consider St. John of the Cross as a representative of a sane and balanced Christianity and not simply as a reflection of a distorted historical epoch?

These objections are not without merit. However, historically, they contradict the process by which Christianity acted as the ferment of the national spirit, molding it in tandem with the historical circumstances of the age. The spirituality of a nation of warriors, clerics, and peasants will be markedly different from that of a society composed of bourgeoisie and proletariat. Nevertheless, in spite of different historical configurations, the mystery of the Church, resounding in different voices from the time of the Apostles to the present can be faithfully reflected. It is not out of the question to affirm that the thought of St. John of the Cross is an authentic reflection of this mystery.

During his lifetime criticism was at least as severe and far more dangerous. This is evidenced by Fray Basilio Ponce de León's defense of the Saint's work. The basic charge was "illuminism," the texts examined by the Holy Office (the Inquisition) were taken from the *Subida* (The Ascent of Mount Carmel), and the *Noche* (The Dark Night).[1] Fray Basilio was an Augustinian Friar who occupied the prestigious Chair of Prime at the University of Salamanca, a cousin of the illustrious Fray Luis de León. His defense of Fray Juan took the form of forty propositions and was dated July 11, 1622.

The Inquisitorial examiners faulted the notion of detachment, which they interpreted as an incitement to those interior motions that open the door to libidinous actions and encourage abstention from good and obligatory works. They found traces of the iconoclastic beliefs of the Illuminati as well as their belief that charitable works are not done for the love of God and that libidinous acts can be considered an effect of the spirit. Moreover, the Inquisitors believed there might be a link between the Saint's thought and that of the Illuminati of Seville, who believed themselves to be sinless and confirmed in

---

1. "Reply of R.P.M. Fray Basilio Ponce de León," in *The Complete Works of St. John of the Cross* (Westminister: Newman, 1945), 3:382-434.

grace.[2] A further resemblance was noted to the Illuminati of Melo, who formulated their beliefs in the language of love, teaching that in the state of "relaxation," prayer, recollection, and other pious practices were unnecessary.

Fray Basilio remarks:[3]

> What is happening with regard to this book in connection with the Illuminati of Seville happened also, at the time of the Illuminati of Llerena and Jaen, in connection with the book entitled the Ascent of Mount Sion.

Fray Bernardino de Laredo's book was investigated by the Holy Office and cleared of all suspicion. It was a favorite of St. Teresa.

Fray Basilio, in his energetic defense, noted that Fray Juan de la Cruz' works had been approved by learned theologians as well as by the University of Alcalá. Not only was his life blameless, he also was one of the founders of the Discalced Carmelite Friars. His close relationship to "the holy Mother Teresa" is stressed, indicating that the Discalced Carmelite Order had initiated proceedings to secure his beatification, a process that would be aborted should the Holy Office prohibit the work. In addition, the Saint's flesh was incorrupt and his relics favored by miracles.

St. John's doctrine is firmly Catholic and of great profit for the few souls whom God leads on this road to perfection. Unfortunately, many misconceptions have arisen through not reading his works in context and condemning certain doctrines simply because the Illuminati parrot certain of his thoughts. Fray Basilio buttresses his defense with a lengthy catalogue of authorities: from St. Augustine and St. Gregory through St. Thomas Aquinas to St. Teresa and the Jesuit theologian Francisco Suárez. In a caustic aside to the examiners, he remarks that "if a man, however learned he be, cannot comprehend the

---

2. "Reply," Nos. 11, 18, 20, 28, 30-32, 34; *Complete Works*, ed. Peers, 3:390-91, 402, 404-405, 413-14, 416, 420, 422.

3. "Reply," No. 6, *Complete Works*, ed. Peers, 3:385-89.

subtleties of this kind of prayer he should not desire the condemnation of books which teach it to those who are capable of practicing it."[4]

The Inquisition is barely mentioned by St. John in his works, though it was an ever-present nuisance that both he and St. Teresa had to take into account. The fact that he destroyed documents before being carted off to the Toledo prison and immediately prior to his death at Úbeda, might well point to fear of the Inquisition or possibly to the then-incipient persecution of the Discalced by the Calced Friars. Perhaps like Mother Teresa he considered the Holy Office a disturbing but not wholly unwelcome presence that could be placated, cajoled, influenced and, possibly, circumvented.[5]

It often seems that the Inquisition was an organization gone wild. Many saintly persons were among those accused of Illuminism and other "crimes." These included the Bl. Juan de Ávila, St. Ignatius Loyola, Fray Luis de Granada, St. Teresa, and St. John of the Cross. The fear of Lutheranism from the outside, *converso* agitation from the inside, and the proliferation of bizarre sects seemed to justify the presence of the Holy Office, an autochthonous Spanish entity. These sects were known as *alumbrados, iluminados,* and *dexados,* with roots extending back to the Albigensians of Catalonia and the Beghards of Valencia, which acted as the ground of outbursts in the fifteenth century and which resurfaced with a vengeance in the sixteenth.[6]

As is to be expected, bizarre incidents proliferated. A Franciscan Friar of Ocaña deluded himself into believing that he had been favored by a revelation commanding him to copulate with "holy women" so as to breed prophets. In 1529 a conventical of *alumbrados* was uncovered who taught that the love of God in humankind is God, that in *dexamiento* (ecstasy) perfect freedom and sinlessness is attained. Far more intriguing were the *alumbrados* of Llerena who practiced lengthy prayer and meditation on the wounds of Christ, which produced orgias-

4. "Reply," Nos. 1-10; *Complete Works,* ed. Peers, 3:385-89.
5. For St. Teresa's jousts with the Inquisition, see Efrén de la Madre de Dios, OCD, and Otger Steggink, OCM, *Tiempo y Vida de Santa Teresa* (Madrid: BAC, 1968).
6. Marcelino Menéndez y Pelayo, *Historia de los Heterodoxos Españoles* (Madrid: BAC, 1956), 2:170ff.

tic movements called "melting in the love of God" — which in turn, they believed, rendered them incapable of sinning. The contagion spread to Seville about the year 1563 reaching an absurd peak with Padre Francisco Méndez who, after celebrating Mass, participated in nude liturgical dancing. He must have been a man of great charisma as he reportedly once celebrated a Mass that lasted for no less than twenty-three hours.[7]

The less scandalous and far more intellectual vein of illuminism reached its zenith years after St. John's demise in the *Guida Spirituale* of Miguel de Molinos, published at Rome in 1675. Although first judged to be orthodox it was later condemned in part due to the intrigues of the French Ambassador. In November 1687, Pope Innocent XI signed a Bull condemning sixty-eight propositions from the *Guida* and Molinos' unpublished writings. This was not the work of the Spanish Inquisition. It should be remembered that, in spite of its manifest abuses and guilt in lowering the spiritual and intellectual tone of Spain, it was the Inquisition that preserved the nation from the witch-hysteria which devastated middle Europe, probably causing more casualties than the autos-da-fé.[8]

*   *   *

Miracles, marvels, prodigies, relic-worship, and diabolical manifestations are popularly supposed to have characterized the Middle Ages and its Iberian sixteenth-century extension. Although basically a caricature, it carries a portion of truth. King Philip II had a large collection of relics that included over one hundred heads, and he was not by any means the prime collector among European monarchs. The so-called 'leyenda negra' (black legend) fabricated in Venice and propagated by London supplied additional somber notes to the already dark portrait. The Inquisition seen through the distorted prism of Juan Antonio Llorente,[9] the heavy-handed rule of the Duke of Alba in the Netherlands, and a

---

7. *Ibid.*, 173-77, 188-89f., 195.

8. Henry Kamen, *The Spanish Inquisition* (New York: Mentor, 1968), 203-9.

9. Juan Antonio Llorente gave a biased and greatly exaggerated account of the Spanish Inquisition because of his Francophile liberal leanings. *Historia Crítica de la Inquisición en España* (Madrid: Hiperion, 1981), 4 vols.

hundred other unpleasant details completed the picture. One must ask: Where does St. John of the Cross stand regarding the reality undergirding these accusations?

In the spring of 1585 Fray Juan de la Cruz initiated a period of activity that would last until the summer of 1588, motivated by a trip to Lisbon from Granada to a chapter convened by Fray Jerónimo Gracián. There, he was elected Definitor and Doria Provincial. While he was at Lisbon, a fellow Carmelite urged him to visit Sor María de la Visitación, "the nun of the wounds," who reportedly had been favored with stigmata, raptures, and levitations, and who merited the approval of eminent churchmen. Fray Juan refused outright: "Why go to see a fraud . . . you will see that the Lord will uncover the deception." On returning to Granada he discovered that his *socius* had returned burdened with relics of the miraculous nun. Fray Juan ordered him to throw them away posthaste. When asked by the Friars at Los Mártires — the Granada monastery — the reason for his lack of interest: "I did not want to see her. . . . I would think very little of my faith if I thought it would increase because of such things."[10]

Sor Isabel de San Jerónimo suffered from a malady that baffled the physicians; she was also thought to be possessed. Fray Juan was sent to initiate an exorcism. After hearing her confession and examining her, he informed the Superior that "this sister does not have a demon, simply lack of judgment," recommending more sleep and change of diet.[11] A troubled woman, one of those pious souls who center their life around church functions, "Madre Peñuela" believed that she was persecuted by the Devil: she would fall on the floor and it would be nearly impossible to move her. Fray Juan gave her a discipline (a whip) with which to castigate herself when attacked by the Devil. The persecution ceased.[12] In a more sophisticated age this would be viewed as a prime example of psychological legerdemain. The Saint's sense of humor was, it seems, not that highly developed.

10. Crisógono de Jesús Sacramentado, OCD, and Matías del Niño Jesús, OCD, *Vida y Obras Completas de San Juan de la Cruz, Doctor de la Iglesia Universal* (Madrid: BAC, 1960), 288-90.

11. *Ibid.*, 122.

12. *Ibid.*, 204-5.

Although other examples of his expertise can be provided, it must be conceded that he cannot be totally disengaged from the foibles of his age. The Concordances of his works dedicate no less than eight pages to the Devil in whom he believed as well as in the possibility of his making pacts with human beings.[13] Examples can be given of this side of his character. A nun at the Augustinian convent of Nuestra Señora de Gracia was credited with possessing an extraordinary grasp of Scripture without any formal education. Eminent theologians such as Fray Juan de Guevara and Fray Luis de León had examined her and approved her spirit. In spite of this, Mother Teresa and the General of the Augustinian Order asked Fray Juan to examine the nun. He did so and concluded that she was possessed and a lengthy, arduous, and grisly exorcism was initiated which was to last several months.[14]

Another case, though not so clear, is that of Juana Calancha, a one-time Discalced Carmelite nun who might have been at one point under the Saint's direction. She was accused of bizarre behavior of a scandalous erotic nature, expelled from the convent, and later penanced by the Murcian Inquisition with a hundred lashes.[15] A problem remains: was she actually under his direction? Could he have been remiss in his duty? Or perhaps deceived?

*　　*　　*

In his works St. John of the Cross is abundantly clear. He recognizes the existence of supernatural phenomena, some of which he experienced. Raptures, ecstasies, and so forth go beyond the usual boundaries of nature and can be accompanied by phenomena such as cataleptic rigidity and anesthesia. While the delight can be immense, the pain can reach the level of torture, to the point of causing dislocated bones.[16] He was extremely suspicious of exhibitions that mimic sanctity, which he

13. Fray Luis de San José, OCD, *Concordancias de las Obras y Escritos del Doctor de la Iglesia San Juan de la Cruz* (Burgos: Editorial Monte Carmelo, 1980), 360-67.

14. Crisógono, *Vida y Obras*, 117-18.

15. *Ibid.*, 209-10. See "aclaración," 219-20.

16. *Cántico*, XIV.19; XIII.4; XXI.16; *Llama*, III.5.

thought could be aided by the Devil. In any case, the delights of the world pale compared to that suavity of the spirit, which "makes the soul taste . . . of eternal life."[17] These extraordinary experiences, the Saint insists, should never be desired nor should attempts be made to procure them.

He believed in the possibility of miracles but tilted to the hard-nosed when faced with concrete instances. They should be attentively considered, as frauds abound. In any case, paying too much attention to the miraculous detaches the soul from the substantial habit of faith. When God is served without the testimony of signs and miracles faith is far greater and more to be extolled.[18] The joy that is generated by marvelous events should be displaced to God. It is far better to suffer for God than to work miracles.

*   *   *

The Saint in his youth was known for his rigorous penitential life. With aging he mellowed, especially insofar as others were concerned, acidly criticizing those superiors and individuals who imposed severe penances while downgrading obedience:[19]

> there are persons without reason who postpone . . . obedience, which is the penitence of reason . . . to corporeal penance . . . which is no more than the penitence of beasts.

Penance is merely a means to an end, not an end itself. The end, the goal, is self-denial, nicely expressed by an acute maxim: "humble is he who hides himself in his own nothingness and knows how to cast himself upon God."[20] Self-negation is the necessary prologue to the ascent of the mystical Mount Carmel.

17. *Cántico*, VI.3; *Llama*, I.6.
18. *Subida*, III.30.4; III.31.3-4; III.31.8.
19. *Noche*, I.6.1-2.
20. "Other Maxims," in *Complete Works*, ed. Peers, 3:259.

St. John of the Cross was an exceptional psychologist. This is not a pious exaggeration, icing on the hagiographic cake. In a manner reminiscent of Freud but *a lo divino,* he takes an inconsequential phenomenon and traces it back to its origins or forward to its consequences. For example, he takes "delight in touch" and views it as the cause of spiritual and moral defects. The Saint begins with "delight in touching fine materials," and views it as leading to a reduction in religious observances, a lessening of adequate corporeal penance, ultimately to contempt for those who dress differently and even hatred of the poor and humble.[21]

Individuals should not delight in anything except God, and to attain the goal of union the will must be darkened and purged of delight in sensible things as this ineluctably leads to imperfections, if not vices. Hearing to distraction, taste to gluttony, tact to vain joy. Notwithstanding, a strange metamorphosis can take place. In rejecting delight in sensible things, the sensual can become spiritual and the animal, rational.[22]

Fray Juan had little sympathy for eccentrics and eccentricities. He derides those mawkishly pious people who burden themselves with medals, relics and the like, comparing them to children playing with trinkets. The use of "curious rosaries" also draws his criticism, admonishing the pious to place their delight not on those objects but rather in the living reality which they represent. Those who place their devotion in dressing and ornamenting statues oblivious of what they represent transform them into idols.[23]

At a far remove from the contemporary pursuit of pleasure and the religion of healthy-mindedness, St. John of the Cross was always following the path of *la cruz a secas,* the cross unadorned. His constant teaching: "the way of suffering is more certain than that of enjoyment."[24] The most pure suffering causes a more intimate and purer un-

---

21. *Subida,* III.25.8.
22. *Subida,* III.24.2–III.26.3.
23. *Noche,* I.3.1; *Subida,* III.25.2; III.35.4.
24. *Noche,* II.16.9.

derstanding of God as well as a purer and more elevated joy. In sum: the cross is the only bridge to eternal happiness.

*   *   *

The lament that the world is growing old is itself as old as civilization and has been used to good effect by a great number of luminaries including Cicero and St. Augustine. This could with good reason be applied to the present epoch, a period of transition, which, to cite Martin Heidegger, is the time of the gods that have fled and the God that is coming.[25] This historical parenthesis characterized in its beginnings by the proliferation of Existentialism, a philosophy befitting a time of crisis, inaugurated in a serious vein by Heidegger's dense *Sein und Zeit,* on a popular level captivated the public consciousness through the novels and plays of Jean-Paul Sartre and his followers. The notions they propagated on alienation, anguish, forlornness, despair, the sense of being thrown into the world, and so on, became familiar terms not only in intellectual circles but also on the cocktail circuit.

In a way, St. John of the Cross and other mystics of the same stripe can be considered as anticipating existential themes. A point is reached in the ascent to God when God withdraws, is ostensibly absent, and the individual soul actually experiences the absence of God depicted in the Psalms of David and Solomon. This can become intolerable and is expressed in forceful terms such as terror, horror, anguish, and fear. Entrance into the dark night brings about the terrifying presence of God's absence, a state in which the soul remains in continual groaning, alone in darkness, so constricted that if God would not provide those approaching perfection would die.[26] St. John of the Cross, then, at least provisionally, is more of an atheist than the atheistic existentialist. He indicates that the soul suffers like Jonas in the belly of the whale, in darkness and anguish, blasted by the abomination which Isa-

25. "Hölderlin on the Essence of Poetry," in *Existence and Being,* ed. W. Brock (London: Vision Press, 1949), 319.

26. *Cántico,* I.14; I.22; XI.9.

iah called the *spiritus-vertiginis,* one of the worst horrors which stalk the night.[27]

There is, of course, a vast difference between the existentialist malaise and the terrors of the mystic. The horrible night of contemplation with all its fear and trembling is not an end in itself, the last spiral of the lost soul into despair or psychosis or a definitive "no exit." On the contrary, it is the purgation necessary to elevate the soul to union with God. The terrors lead to happiness and joy. The Saint advises us to elevate our hearts to God in happiness and joy as God has in Himself every beauty and grace.[28]

27. *Noche,* I.14.3-12; II.6.1; II.7.3. From Isaiah 43:14: "The Lord has infused into them a spirit that warps their judgment" (NET).

28. *Subida,* III.21.2; *Noche,* II.1.1; II.15.2; *Cántico,* XVI.6; XIV.18.

Epilogue

To benefit from the works of St. John of the Cross deeply and spiritually, it is first necessary to possess an adamantine Christian faith and scrupulous personal honesty, both very hard to come by. Can we dismiss those early morning doubts that plague us, and the fantasies that hold us in thrall? Or can we look in the mirror and actually see our authentic faces, the faces God sees and not those caricatures we have lovingly concocted?

Even for our less-than-perfect selves the reading of St. John's works can be a memorable experience in more ways than simply appreciating the intellectual and aesthetic value of his thought. A process of stripping analogous but scarcely similar to that experienced by those privileged souls ascending Mount Carmel may occur. The reader can discover a coil of hypocrisy, self-delusion, and malice slithering out of the innermost self while a further coil begins to solidify and waits its turn. It follows that a certain self-criticism even self-disgust can well up in the reader. Albeit unpleasant in itself, these attitudes favor understanding the text as well as furthering the spiritual growth of the individual.

As repeated perhaps *ad nauseam* in this study, St. John of the Cross belonged to a world vastly different from our twenty-first century world. His radical, single-minded pursuit of God floats uneasily in the atheistic, agnostic, or religiously trivial consciousness of the present age. Our categories do not apply. Penitence, silence, prayer, meditation, contemplation, and a multitude of other things are today dismissed as atavistic intruders in the world of instant gratification.

This frank distaste for everything represented by the Saint stems from his opposition to the "good things" of the contemporary world. He insists that a humanity attempting to usurp the attributes of Divinity is scarcely what it is called to be: the new self preached by Saint Paul; and that the conception of a material universe growing progressively more awesome to the point of overshadowing the God-Man who died on the cross must be rejected. This Behemoth is itself a creature composed of creatures and is hence in debt to its Creator. In contrast to the *Grand être,* a deified humanity, St. John of the Cross teaches that our being is rooted in God, bound to Him from within: "His countenance filled with the graces of all creation, awesome in power and glory."[1]

St. John's thought, partially because of its alien character, requires a lengthy process of intellectual and spiritual assimilation. A mindless plunge into his works is not advisable. It can lead to serious misconceptions. For the neophyte, in fact for most of us, a point is reached in which the text becomes a succession of disconnected sounds that, like sparks, dazzle and vanish in the air. Other difficulties arise because of the distance that separates us from that Reality which transcends our minuscule world and always *is.* Enmeshed as we are in the maelstrom of everyday life, St. John has much to teach us: how to arrive at a permanent shelter.

Perhaps the best way of assessing the value of Sanjuanist thought is to compare it to that of another Christian religious thinker of note, St. Augustine. Maurice Blondel praised him for[2]

the moving tones, the glowing imagery, the splendor of spiritual vision, all continue to form a whole which, viewed from without, impress the spectator as something unique, like the beauty of a masterpiece of art.

1. *Llama,* IV.11.
2. Maurice Blondel, "The Latent Resources in St. Augustine's Thought," *A Monument to Saint Augustine* (London: Sheed & Ward, 1945), 319-20.

In such a disparate personality as St. John of the Cross much of this eulogy is not applicable.

Where Augustine states his case forcibly and clearly, John hints about a domain that transcends rational categories. As a poet his glorious imagery and moving tones are aesthetically mindboggling, but they are not carried over to the commentaries, fairly unexciting decodings of his verse. Augustine is primarily a thinker, a superb one, in spite of his mystical leanings.[3] John's prose is colorless, repetitive, lacking *élan* except for a few random but striking passages.

While Augustine takes the path of knowing, John moves along the path of unknowing. Augustine endeavors to know God as far as reason allows and then, if possible, take a leap to a higher level of reality. John employs reason in its philosophical mode principally to clarify, to remove obstacles to the ascent, to teach the path to holiness. While Augustine views aseity (that is, self-existence) as the prime Divine Attribute in spite of his glorious words regarding beauty, John chooses beauty. Both are lovers of solitude and interiority of prayer, following in the steps of their Lord, who, the Gospels tell us, withdrew for solitary prayer in the still of the night, to mountaintops and the wilderness.

Edith Stein, a modern-day Discalced Carmelite and martyr, stated: "to stand before the face of the living God — that is our vocation. . . . St. John, like Elijah, stood before God's face because this was the eternal treasure for whose sake he gave up all earthly goods."[4] This was his genius. The rest is commentary.

3. My "Augustine: Spiritual Centaur?" *Augustine: Mystic and Mystagogue*, ed. Frederick Van Fleteren, Joseph C. Schnaubelt, OSA, and Joseph Reino (New York: Peter Lang, 1994), 159-76.

4. Stein, *The Hidden Life* (Washington: ICS, 1992), 1-2.

Select Bibliography

Primary Sources

The Collected Works of Saint John of the Cross. Translated by Kieran Kavanaugh, OCD, and Otilio Rodriguez, OCD. 2nd edition. Washington: ICS Publications, 1973.

The Complete Works of St. John of the Cross. Translated and edited by E. Allison Peers. 3 vols. London: Burns, Oates & Washbourne Ltd., 1953.

Concordancias de las Obras y Escritos del Doctor de la Iglesia San Juan de la Cruz. Edited by Fray Luis de San José, OCD. Burgos: Monte Carmelo, 1980.

Jerónimo de San José, OCD. *Historia del Venerable Padre Fray Juan de la Cruz.* Madrid, 1641.

José de Jesús María (Quiroga), OCD. *Historia de la vida y virtudes del Venerable P. Fray Juan de la Cruz.* Brussels, 1628.

Crisógono de Jesús Sacramentado, OCD, and Matías del Niño Jesús, OCD. *Vida y Obras Completas de San Juan de la Cruz, Doctor de la Iglesia Universal.* Critical edition and notes by Licinio del S. S. Sacramento, OCD. Madrid: BAC, 1960.

Peers, E. Allison. *Handbook of the Life and Times of St. Teresa and St. John of the Cross.* London: Burns, Oates & Washbourne Ltd., 1954.

Silverio de Sta. Teresa, OCD. *Obras de San Juan de la Cruz Doctor de la Iglesia. Editadas y Anotadas.* 5 vols. Burgos: Monte Carmelo, 1929-1931.

———. *San Juan de la Cruz.* Vol. 5 of *Historia del Carmen Descalzo en España, Portugal y América.* Burgos: Monte Carmelo, 1936.

Secondary Sources

Ballesteros, Manuel. *Juan de la Cruz.* Barcelona: Ediciones Península, 1977.

Bard, André. *Memorie et Espèrance chez Jean de la Croix.* Paris: Beauchesne, 1971.

Baruzi, Jean. *Saint Jean de la Croix et le problème de l'expérience mystique.* Paris: Alcan, 1924.

———. "Introduction à la Recherches sur la Langage Mystique." In *Recherches Philosophiques.* Paris: Bovin, 1932.

Brennan, Gerald. *St. John of the Cross.* Cambridge: Cambridge University Press, 1973.

Bruno de Jesús-Marie, OCD. *St. John of the Cross.* Edited by Benedict Zimmerman, OCD. New York: Sheed & Ward, 1932.

———, ed. *Three Mystics.* London: Sheed & Ward, 1952.

Chevalier, Dom Philippe. *Saint Jean de la Croix.* Paris: Aubier, 1958.

Crisógono de Jesús Sacramentado, OCD. *San Juan de la Cruz: su obra científica y su obra literaria.* 2 vols. Madrid: Mensajero, 1929.

———. *La Escuela Mística Carmelitana.* Madrid: Mensajero, 1930.

Dalbiez, Roland. *Saint Jean de la Croix d'ápres M. Baruzi.* Paris: Desclée, 1928.

Dombrowski, Daniel A. *St. John of the Cross: An Appreciation.* Albany: State University of New York Press, 1992.

Dubay, Thomas, S.M. *Fire Within.* San Francisco: Ignatius, 1989.

Frost, Bede. *Saint John of the Cross.* London: Hodder & Stoughton, 1937.

Morel, George. *Le Sens de l'Existence selon S. Jean de la Croix.* 3 vols. Paris: Aubier, 1961.

de Nicolas, Antonio T. *St. John of the Cross: Alchemist of the Soul.* New York: Paragon House, 1989.

Ruiz Salvador, Federico, OCD. *Introducción a San Juan de la Cruz*. Madrid: BAC, 1968.

Sanson, Henri. *El Espíritu Humano según San Juan de la Cruz*. Madrid: Rialp, 1962.

Stein, Edith. *The Science of the Cross*. Translated by Hilda Graef. Chicago: Henry Regnery, 1960.

————. *The Hidden Life*. Washington: ICS Publications, 1992.

Wojtyla, Karol. *Faith According to St. John of the Cross*. Translated by Jordan Aumann. San Francisco: Ignatius, 1981. (Translation into Spanish by Alvaro Huerga. Madrid: BAC, 1979.)

Related Works

Alonso, Dámaso. *La poesía de San Juan de la Cruz*. Madrid: Aguilar, 1942.

Asin Palacios, Miguel. *Huellas del Islam*. Madrid: Espasa, 1941.

von Balthasar, Hans Urs. *The Glory of God: A Theological Aesthetics*. Translated by A. Louth, J. Saward, A. Simon, and R. Williams. Edited by John Richer. 3 vols. San Francisco: Ignatius, 1986.

Bataillon, Marcel. *Erasme et l'Espagne*. Paris, 1937.

————. "Sur la genese poetique du Cantique Spirituel." *Boletin del Instituto Vaso y Cuervo* 3 (1949).

A Benedictine of Stanbrook Abbey. *Medieval Mystical Tradition and St. John of the Cross*. London: Burns & Oates, 1954.

Bouyer, Louis. *The Christian Mystery*. Translated by Illtyd Trethowan. Edinburgh: T&T Clark, 1990.

Butler, Dom Cuthbert, OSB. *Western Mysticism*. London: Arrow, 1960.

Campbell, Roy. *The Poems of St. John of the Cross*. London: Harvill, 1953.

Dicken, E. W. Trueman. *The Crucible of Love*. London: Darton, Longman & Todd, 1963.

Farrer, Austin. *The Glass of Vision*. Westminster: Dacre Press, 1966.

Hatzfeld, Helmut. *Estudios literarios sobre mística española*. Madrid: Gredos, 1955.

Jones, C., G. Wainwright, and E. Yarnold, SJ, eds. *The Study of Spirituality*. New York: Oxford University Press, 1986.

Leclercq, Dom Jean, OSB. *Aux Sources de la Spiritualité Occidental.* Paris: Editions du Cerf, 1964.

——. OSB, F. Vandenbroucke, and L. Bouyer. *The Spirituality of the Middle Ages.* London: Burns & Oates, 1968.

de Lubac, Henri. *The Mystery of the Supernatural.* Translated by Rosemary Sheed. New York: Sheed & Ward, 1967.

Mascall, E. L. *Words & Images.* London: Longmans, Green, 1957.

McNabb, Vincent M., OP. "The Mysticism of St. John of the Cross." Blackfriars (reprint).

Peers, E. Allison. *Studies in the Spanish Mystics.* 2 vols. London: The Sheldon Press, 1927-30.

Rubio, David, OSA. *La "fonte" de San Juan de la Cruz.* La Habana: Minerva, 1946.

——. *La Filosofía del Quijote.* Buenos Aires: Editorial Losada, 1943.

Sheils, W. J., ed. *Monks, Hermits and the Ascetic Tradition.* London: Blackwell, 1985.

Tavard, George. *Poetry and Contemplation in St. John of the Cross.* Athens, Ohio: Ohio University Press, 1988.

Thibon, Gustave. *Nietzsche ou le Déclin de L'Esprit.* Paris: Fayard, 1975.

Vilnet, Jean. *Bible et Mystique chez Saint Jean de la Croix.* Paris: Desclée de Brouwer, 1949.

Appendix

I am presenting here the text and a translation of *The Living Flame of Love*, *The Dark Night*, and thirteen of the forty stanzas of *The Spiritual Canticle* as an aid to the understanding of the present work, and no more. There exist a multiplicity of translations of the Saint's poetic oeuvre to which the reader can refer with profit (see bibliography). Personally, I am attempting to steer a course between Rodriguez/Kavanaugh, Roy Campbell, and Allison Peers, opting for simplicity over style.

Appendix

Llama (The Living Flame of Love)

1. ¡Oh, Llama de amor viva,
   Que tiernamente hieres
   de mi alma en el más profundo centro!;
   pues ya no eres esquiva,
   acaba ya, si quieres;
   rompe la tela de este dulce encuentro.

   Oh, flame of living love
   That you tenderly wound
   My soul in its most profound center!
   As you are no longer elusive,
   Finish now if you wish;
   Break the web of this sweet encounter.

2. ¡Oh, cauterio suave!
   ¡Oh regalada llaga!
   ¡Oh mano blanda! ¡Oh toque delicado,
   Que a vida eterna sabe
   y toda deuda paga!
   Matando, muerte en vida la has trocado.

   Oh, sweet cautery!
   Oh, delectable wound!
   Oh, soft hand! Oh, delicate touch!
   That tastes of eternal life
   And pays every debt!
   Slaying, you transform death into life.

3. ¡Oh, lámparas de fuego,
   en cuyos resplandores
   las profundas cavernas del sentido
   que estaba oscuro y ciego,
   con extraños primores
   calor y luz dan junto a su Querido!

   Oh, lamps of fire,
   In their refulgence
   The profound caverns of sensibility
   That were dark and blind
   With strange beauty
   Give heat and light together with their
   Beloved.

4. ¡Cuán manso y amoroso
   recuerdas en mi seno,
   donde secretamente solo moras,
   y en tu aspirar sabroso
   de bien y gloria lleno
   cuán delicadamente me enamoras!

   How gently and lovingly
   You remain in my heart,
   Where you also sweetly dwell
   And in your delightful breathing
   Full of goodness and glory
   How delicately you romance me!

Cántico Espiritual (Spiritual Canticle)

1. Bride

¿Adónde te escondiste	Where have you hidden
amado, y me dejaste con gemido?	Beloved, and left me moaning?
como el ciervo huiste,	Like the stag you fled,
habiéndome herido;	Having wounded me;
salí tras ti clamando y eras ido.	I followed crying but you were gone.

4. Question to all Creatures

¡Oh bosques y espesuras,	Oh, forests and thickets,
plantadas por la mano del Amado,	Planted by the hand of the beloved,
oh prado de verduras,	Oh field of verdures,
de flores esmaltado!	Enameled with flowers!
decid si por vosotros ha pasado.	Tell if by you He has passed.

5. Reply of the Creatures

Mil gracias derramando,	A thousand graces showering,
pasó por estos sotos con presura,	He passed in haste among these groves,
y yéndolos mirando,	And glancing at them,
con sola su figura	With his visage alone
vestidos los dejó de hermosura.	Left them garbed in beauty.

6. Bride

Ay, ¿quién podrá sanarme?	Oh, who is able to cure me?
acaba de entregarte ya de vero,	Finish surrendering yourself fully,
no quieras enviarme	Do not wish to send me
de hoy más mensajero	From today more messengers
que no saben decirme lo que quiero.	Who cannot tell me what I burn for.

7. Bride

Y todos cuantos vagan,	And all those who wander,
de ti me van mil gracias refiriendo	Recount of you a thousand graces
y todos más me llagan,	All of which injures more,
y déjanme muriendo	Leaving me dying
un no sé qué que quedan balbuciendo.	Not knowing what they keep stammering.

11. Bride

Descubre tu presencia,	Reveal your presence
y máteme tu vista y hermosura;	And slay me with your sight and beauty;
mira que la dolencia	Look, the sickness
de amor, que no se cura	of love cannot be cured
sino con la presencia y la figura.	Save only by the presence and the visage.

12. Bride

¡Oh, cristalina fuente,	Oh, crystalline fount,
si en esos tu semblantes plateados,	If only in your silvered countenance
formases de repente	Would suddenly form
los ojos deseados,	Those desired orbs
que tengo en mis entrañas dibujados!	Which in my inmost heart are sketched!

13. Bridegroom

Vuélvete, paloma	Return, dove
que el ciervo vulnerado	The wounded stag
por el otero asoma,	Appears on the knoll
al aire de tu vuelo, y fresco toma.	To the air of your flight, and is refreshed.

14. Bride

Mi Amado, las montañas,	My love, the mountains,
los valles solitarios nemorosos,	The solitary sylvan valleys,
las ínsulas extrañas,	The strange and distant lands,
los ríos sonorosos,	The sonorous rivers,
el silbo de los aires amorosos.	The whistle of the amorous breezes.

15. Bride

La noche sosegada	The calm night
en par de los levantes del aurora,	Announcing the advent of the dawn,
la música callada,	The silent music,
la soledad sonora,	The sounding solitude,
la cena que recrea y enamora.	The dinner that delights and enamors.

26. Bride

En la interior bodega
de mi Amado bebí, y cuando salía
por toda aquesta vega,
ya cosa no sabía,
y el ganado perdí, que antes seguía.

In the inner cellar
of my Beloved I drank, and emerging
Throughout that plain,
I knew nothing,
And lost the cattle which I followed.

35. Bridegroom

En soledad vivía,
y en soledad ha puesto ya su nido,
y en soledad la guía
a solas su querido,
también en soledad de amor herido.

In solitude she lived,
In solitude she put her nest,
In solitude He guides
Alone his beloved,
In solitude of wounded love.

36. Bride

Gocémonos, Amado,
y vámonos a ver en tu hermosura
al monte o al collado,
do mana el agua pura;
entremos más adentro en la espesura.

Let us rejoice, Beloved
And we shall see in your beauty
To mountain or to hill,
Where flows the purest water;
And pass further into the woods.

Noche Oscura (The Dark Night)

1. En una noche oscura,
   con ansias, en amores inflamada,
   ¡oh dichosa ventura!
   salí sin ser notada,
   estando ya mi casa sosegada;

2. A oscuras, y segura
   por la secreta escala, disfrazada,
   ¡oh dichosa ventura!
   a oscuras y en celada,
   estando ya mi casa sosegada;

3. en la Noche dichosa,
   en secreto, que nadie me veía,
   ni yo miraba cosa,
   sin otra luz y guía,
   sino la que en el corazón ardía.

4. Aquésta me guiaba
   más cierto que la luz del mediodía,
   adonde me esperaba
   quien yo bien me sabía
   en parte donde nadie parecía.

5. ¡Oh Noche que guiaste!
   ¡Oh Noche amable más que la alborada!
   ¡Oh Noche que juntaste
   amado con amada,
   amada en el Amado transformada!

6. En mi pecho florido,
   que entero para él solo se guardaba,
   allí quedó dormido,
   y yo le regalaba,
   y el ventalle de cedros aire daba.

On one dark night,
With cares inflamed in love,
Oh!, the sheer grace
I went abroad unseen,
when all my house was hushed;

In darkness, and secure
By the secret stair, disguised,
Oh! The sheer grace
In darkness and concealed,
My house now being stilled;

Upon that fortunate night,
In secret, unseen,
Nor did I look at anything,
With no other light nor guide,
Save that which in my heart was burning.

This guided me
More surely than the light of noon,
To where One waited near
Whose presence well I knew
There where no one else appeared.

Oh, night that was my guide!
Oh, night more lovely than the dawn!
Oh, night that has united
Lover and Beloved
Transforming each into the other!

Within my flowering breast,
Kept solely for Himself alone,
He sank into His sleep,
And I regarded Him,
Lulled by the breeze from the cedars.

7. El aire del almena,
   cuando yo sus cabellos esparcía,
   con su mano serena
   en mi cuello hería
   y todos mis sentidos suspendía.

8. Quedéme y olvidéme,
   el rostro recliné sobre el Amado:
   cesó todo y dejéme,
   dejando mi cuidado
   entre las azucenas olvidado.

Over the ramparts fanned,
When I parted His hair,
With His gentle hand
My neck He wounded
Suspending all my senses.

I remained and forgot myself,
My face reclined on the Beloved:
All ceased and left me,
Leaving my cares
Forgotten among the lilies.

Index

Index

Index

solitude, 8, 80, 88, 98, 101; John's love of, 33, 42, 44, 115-16, 145
Song of Songs, 13, 47, 68, 90, 101, 108
Son of God, 81, 100, 107, 124; as Word, 55, 92, 94, 97
Southern, R. W., 9
Spain: decline of, 22, 24; education in, 25; Golden Age of, 20, 28-29, 66; Islam in, 23, 46; and the Renaissance and Reformation, 20
Spanish Mysticism: A Preliminary Study (Peers), 29
Spinoza, Baruch, 98, 108
Spirit. *See* Holy Spirit
Spirit of Christianity, The (Hegel), 126
Spiritual Exercises (Ignatius), 80, 120
statue metaphor, 54, 69-71
Stein, Edith, 14, 47, 60, 102, 118, 145
stigmata, 137
Stoicism, 8, 59-60
Suárez, Francisco, 120, 134
Subida (John), 33, 45, 51-52, 101, 133; commentary, 75-77, 81-84, 88
suffering, 96, 115, 139-42; caused by God's absence, 51, 58, 93; of John, 17, 90; of Teresa, 31
Sufism, 5
Summa Contra Gentiles (St. Thomas), 129
Summa Theologiae (Thomas Aquinas), 36, 38, 129
supernatural, 17, 53, 80, 82, 85, 111, 120-24, 138
Susán, Diego de, 27
Symonds, Arthur, 57
Symposium (Plato), 11, 72

tabula rasa theory, 38, 62-63
Talavera, Hernando de, 25
Talmud, 5
Tauler, J., 38, 80
Teilhard de Chardin, 118, 121-22, 126
Teresa, Saint, 15, 17, 28-32, 40-42, 45; and

John, 32, 39-42, 59, 134-35, 138; writings of, 1, 40, 94, 97
theology, mystical, 6, 15, 80, 91-92, 100
Thérèse of Lisieux, 14
Thibon, Gustave, 59
Thomas Aquinas, Saint, 17, 36-38, 50, 61-67, 87, 122, 124, 129-31, 134
Thomists, 121
Toledo, 40, 42, 113; John's imprisonment in, 56, 89-90, 112, 135
Torquemada, Tomás de, 23-24, 28
Tostado, Jerónimo, 42
Transfiguration, 82
Trastamara, House of, 22
Triana, Rodrigo de, 25
Trinity, 45, 59, 101, 107

Úbeda, 46, 102, 135
Unamuno, Miguel de, 19-20
Underhill, E., 72
understanding: as faculty of the soul, 53, 78-80, 85-87, 93, 99-101, 105, 109; and faith, 56, 78-79; and God, 72, 91, 105, 129; and knowledge, 97-98, 124; purged, 79, 86-87. *See also* intellect
union with God: and faith, 80; in this life, 79, 99; and love, 58, 97, 104-6; as perfection, 54-55, 76, 108, 110-11; quest for, 7, 50-51, 60, 66, 72, 83-87, 93, 96, 101, 113, 127, 130, 140, 142

Vahanian, Gabriel, 125
Valladolid, 26
Vanneste, Jean, 72
Varieties of Religious Experience (James), 1-2
Vatican Council (Second), 15
Vega, Lope de, 31-32
via illuminativa, 85, 103
Victorines, 7, 15, 38
Victorinus, Marius, 10
Vida (Teresa), 40